The American Diesel
LOCOMOTIVE

Brian Solomon

MBI Publishing Company

Dedication
To my friends, the Hoover family

First published in 2000 by MBI Publishing Company, 729 Prospect Avenue, PO Box 1, Osceola, WI 54020-0001 USA

© Brian Solomon, 2000

MBI Publishing Company books are also available at discounts in bulk quantity for industrial or sales-promotional use. For details write to Special Sales Manager at Motorbooks International Wholesalers & Distributors, 729 Prospect Avenue, PO Box 1, Osceola, WI 54020-0001 USA.

Library of Congress Cataloging-in-Publication Data
Solomon, Brian
      The American diesel locomotive / Brian Solomon.
      p. cm.
      ISBN 0-7603-0666-4 (hbk. : alk. paper)
      1. Diesel locomotives—United States. I. Title.
TJ619.2 S65 2000
625.26'62'0973—dc21   99-050041

On the front cover: This Southern Pacific locomotive was photographed near Castle Rock, Utah. *Brian Solomon*
On the front flap: Santa Fe's "warbonnet" is one of the most recognizable paint schemes in North America. SD75M number 250 was the last new Santa Fe locomotive, delivered in September 1995. *Brian Solomon*
On the frontispiece: This truck detail is of Conrail C30-7A number 6573.
On the title page: A pair of Conrail SD80MACs leads ML-482 (a loaded auto carrier freight) eastbound at Middlefield, Massachusetts, on the morning of October 17, 1997. *Brian Solomon*
On the back cover: At Belmont, Nebraska, a trio of Burlington Northern SD70MACs perform the job they were built for: moving Powder River coal trains. Three SD70MACs replaced five older 3,000 horsepower six-axles in like service. *Brian Solomon*
On the back cover, inset: The difference between EMD's prewar slant nose and the postwar bulldog nose are evident in this period shot taken at the Cincinnati Union Terminal engine house. *Richard Jay Solomon*
On the back flap: A pair of Wisconsin Central SD45s roll through the south switch of the siding at Byron, Wisconsin on March 23, 1996. *Brian Solomon*

Editor-in-Chief: Lee Klancher
Cover design: Dan Perry
Layout Design: Rebecca Allen
Printed in Hong Kong

CONTENTS

Acknowledgments

WRITING THIS BOOK represents the culmination of years experiencing American railroads and diesel-electric locomotives. In that time I have learned from many people about almost every facet of railroading and railroad locomotives. I do not claim to be an expert in any one area of railroading, and I owe much of my knowledge to those with greater expertise than I. This book would not be possible without them.

I would like to thank my father, Richard Jay Solomon, for introducing me to railroads at the earliest age, and for lending me unlimited access to his vast collection of photographs, timetables, and books. Many of the texts used to research this book are from his personal library. In addition, he assisted with photo research and proofreading. Many of the Richard Jay Solomon photographs printed in this book are previously unpublished, and a number of his black and white negatives were specifically printed for use in this text.

My old friends, Tom H. Hoover and Tom S. Hoover, have accompanied me on a variety of trips and excursions, and provided me with their generous hospitality over the years. John Gruber, editor of *Vintage Rails*, has lent his generous support. Sean Graham-White, an acknowledged authority on modern locomotives, was extremely helpful. He assisted with providing source materials, proofreading, and fact checking, in addition to writing two sidebars in Chapter 8. Doug Eisele was very generous with his library of books and photographic collection, and his hospitality. Michael L. Gardner kindly lent me his darkroom facilities. Doug Moore, president of the Amherst Railway Society, helped with copy work and has provided photographic assistance over the years. The Irish Railways Record Society assisted with information on Irish railways, and the EMD diesels that operate there. Robert W. Jones of Pine Tree Press assisted with photo research, and lent me images from the Leon Onofri collection. Robert A. Buck of Tucker's Hobbies in Warren, Massachusetts, has been very helpful over many years, making innumerable introductions, helping with photographs, and random acts of publicity. Tim Doherty has generously provided me historical photographs and drawings from his collection, lent valuable source materials and considerable photographic insight. Thanks to Lori Swingle and Eleanor M. Gehres at the Denver Public Library Western History/Genealogy Department; Bob's Photos of Ansonia, Connecticut; and J.R. Quinn of Worcester, New York, for supplying photographs. Lee Klancher of MBI Publishing has been extremely helpful in the editing and review of the manuscript and discussing ideas for the book. I also thank Robert Foreman for his insight on locomotive operation.

I often travel with other photographers, and I thank all of them for their company and insight that has contributed toward making better images, including: Brian L. Jennison, J.D. Schmid, Mel Patrick, Michael L. Gardner, George S. Pitarys, Mike Abalos, Dean Sauvola, Tom Danneman, Mike Danneman, John Gruber, Dick Gruber, Chris Burger, Scott Bontz, Blair Kooistra, Mark Hemphill, Brian Rutherford, Joe McMillan, Don Gulbrandsen, Doug Moore, Doug Eisele, Mike Schafer, Dave Burton, Don Marson, Gerald Hook, Danny Johnson, F.L Becht, Ed Beaudette, Robert A. Buck, George C. Corey, Howard Ande, Brandon Delaney, Bill Linley, George Melvin, Marshall Beecher, Vic Neves, Emile Tobenfeld, Will Holloway, Hal Miller, John Peters, Norman Yellin, and my brother Seán Solomon. Some have also contributed photographs, and their names are credited in the appropriate captions. I am personally responsible for uncredited photos.

—*Brian Solomon, June 1999*

Twilight at Floy, Utah: a Union Pacific SD40-2 races eastward with a very late *California Zephyr*. The diesel-electric changed the face of American railroads in a short span of time. Today most trains use diesels, but 70 years ago nearly all trains were steam powered, save for those on a few lines where electric power was preferred.

INTRODUCTION

IN THE COURSE of one generation, the diesel engine rose from obscurity to universality. The American railway was born in the 1820s and 1830s, and for the next nine decades the railway locomotive was synonymous with the steam engine. The development of the diesel would completely change this, and a little more than 30 years after the introduction of the first successful diesel locomotives, steam power had been completely purged from American rails. Once the diesel had been proved, it was quickly adopted by most railroads. Although initially a few lines held out, remaining loyal to steam, by 1960, steam had vanished, and diesels were operating across America. This motive power revolution changed the whole nature of the locomotive business from design and construction to sales, application, and maintenance. The traditional steam locomotive manufacturers reluctantly converted from steam production to diesel, but were ill-suited to compete in the new market; a new firm quickly rose to the locomotive forefront. So only a few years after the last steam runs, the last of the traditional builders ended locomotive production.

WHY DIESELIZE?

By the 1940s, the steam locomotive represented more than 125 years of continuous development. Many of the world's most brilliant engineers had spent their lives perfecting and refining the technology. The steam locomotive had progressed from being simple machines weighing just a few tons and capable of hauling just a few wooden wagons, to massive, modern powerhouses with extraordinary output, far more power than was imaginable at the dawn of the railroad era. Chesapeake & Ohio's 2-6-6-6 Allegheny type, first built in 1942, was among the most powerful steam locomotives. It weighed 775,330 pounds, and was capable of producing more than 6,900 horsepower. It could accelerate a 14,000-ton coal train from 0 to 30 miles per hour in just a few minutes on level track.

Several important developments in steam technology had improved locomotive efficiency and allowed for greater power and reduced fuel consumption. The advent of the rear trailing truck in the 1890s permitted a significant enlargement of the locomotive firebox, and therefore a more

Shortly after sunrise on August 31, 1996, near Kennard, Nebraska, Chicago & North Western DASH9-44CW No. 8690 rolls east toward the Missouri River crossing at Blair. Beginning in 1993, C&NW acquired a large fleet of GE DASH9s, followed by a small number of externally similar AC4400CWs. In spring 1995, C&NW merged with Union Pacific, which dispersed C&NW's attractively painted modern GEs across UP's far-flung western rail network.

Electro-Motive's revolutionary FT diesels allowed the railroads to economically dieselize their freight operations. In 1952 a pair of Boston & Maine FTs and a postwar F2A roll past aged 2-8-0 Consolidations destined for the scrap yard. Philip R. Hastings, *Tim Doherty collection*

Opposite
At 6:30 a.m. the silence at Caliente, California, is broken by Santa Fe's 991 roaring upgrade led by a quartet of GE DASH8-40BWs. Two Santa Fe EMDs work as manned midtrain helpers. The California Tehachapis have been described as the 'greatest train watching place in the world.'

powerful locomotive. The introduction of the superheater after the turn of the century improved the overall efficiency of the engine and permitted another significant increase in power. By the end of World War I, most locomotives were equipped with superheaters. Then in the 1920s, the locomotive builders, led by Lima, introduced a whole line of more powerful, efficient locomotives. Lima introduced the twin-axle load-bearing trailing truck, allowing for an even greater expansion of the firebox and boiler. This, in conjunction with other improvements, such as the application of roller bearings to minimize wear, and the use of lightweight reciprocating parts to reduce destructive reciprocating forces known as dynamic augment, led to a whole generation of super-efficient, powerful locomotives.

Why would the railroads consider abandoning a technology that had served them so well for so long, and that had recently made so much progress? What about the diesels made them so compelling?

The railroads had dabbled in motorcar technology, and a few had experimented with electrification. At one time electrification promised to be the power source of the future, but the high initial cost of installation precluded this from becoming a reality in the United States, though it did come to pass primarily in Europe and Japan. The rail motorcar found its place on branchlines and secondary runs. While

One of the many advantages of diesel locomotives over steam was far fewer fueling railroads built elaborate mainline servicing facilities. Chicago & North Western retired its last steam units in the 1950s, but in 1995 its enormous coaling tower at De Kalb, Illinois, still straddled its main line. An eastbound slows for an approach signal at De Kalb on the morning of March 25, 1995.

both technologies found a niche in the industry, neither won widespread acceptance on American railroads. The railroad industry had also experienced its fair share of gimmicks—interesting ideas that didn't work well, or were not cost effective. The non-articulated compound steam locomotive is a good example.

The diesel was more than just a gimmick, and the railroads seriously embraced dieselization for one basic reason: it lowered operating costs. The diesels' numerous benefits all boiled down to basic cost savings. It took a generation, but when the railroads finally realized this, and practical diesel technology had been demonstrated and made available, the steam locomotive was almost universally abandoned. Some lines were quicker than others to embrace the diesel, and a few lines tried to refine steam to a point where it would match the cost-effectiveness of diesels; but ultimately all American railroads discontinued steam operation, converting to diesel—or to be precise, diesel-electric operation—with a few lines maintaining straight electric operations, primarily for heavy suburban passenger services.

Thermal Efficiency

The principal underlying advantage of the diesel engine over the steam engine is superior thermal efficiency. Thermal efficiency is a measure of an engine's effectiveness in converting heat (or potential energy) into power. The reciprocating steam locomotive used an external combustion engine, which suffers from an inherently wasteful conversion of energy to power. By burning its fuel outside the cylinder, the steam engine wastes much of the energy it produces. In an internal combustion diesel engine, however, the fuel is ignited within

On October 23, 1998, Norfolk Southern GE DASH 9-40C 8876 leads empty hoppers west beneath the abandoned coaling tower at Vicker, Virginia. Norfolk & Western was one of many railroads that used expansive mainline fueling facilities to minimize delays; N&W's gigantic Y6 Mallets once paused here for coal. *Tom S. Hoover*

Above: The Missouri Pacific's first locomotive, built in Massachusetts and shipped via sailing vessel and steamboat to St. Louis in 1852. ★ *Below:* One of the several 5400-horsepower Diesel-electric locomotives now hauling freight trains over the Missouri Pacific Lines.

the cylinder or immediately adjacent to it, where much more of the resulting energy may be harnessed. During the nineteenth century, the best steam engines operated at about 6 percent thermal efficiency, a figure that climbed to 10 to 12 percent by the end of the steam era. (The Otto cycle, or spark ignition, engine found in most automobiles operates at about 20 percent thermal efficiency.) The diesel engine achieves an efficiency of between 30 and 35 percent. So even the early diesel-electrics of the mid-1930s were three times more efficient than the most modern steam locomotives.

Fuel Costs

The cost of fuel played an important role in the contest between steam and diesel power. America has enjoyed exceptionally inexpensive petroleum products since the end of World War I, when the gigantic Texas oil fields were discovered. Diesel fuel traditionally has been cheaper than even gasoline. At the time many railroads initially considered diesel locomotives, the price of diesel fuel was about eight cents a gallon. Low fuel cost was a strong incentive for manufacturers and designers to refine the diesel engine.

Traditional steam locomotives typically had to stop about every 100 miles for fuel, and sometimes more often for water. Diesels could operate between 500 and 600 miles between fueling stops. The diesels' greater fuel efficiency and freedom from the need for water meant that railroads could abandon many costly mainline fueling stations, discontinue water stops altogether, and greatly speed up operations. In 1941 Santa Fe tested a four-unit EMD FT set (see Chapter 3) in Chicago to Los Angeles freight service. The diesels only needed to pause five times for fuel and ran the full route, while a typical steam run required at least five locomotive changes and an estimated 35 fuel and water stops. Keeping trains moving, especially at intermediate yards and stations and avoiding stops at intermediate yards and stations, allows for more efficient operations.

Running extra—as indicated by white flags flying on the lead locomotive: an A-B-B-A of Frisco EMD F3s leads a long freight in a scene typical of postwar American railroading. *Tim Doherty collection*

Operational Advantages

Modern steam locomotives typically produced greater horsepower than early diesels, but steam suffered from insufficient power when a locomotive started, and could not generate full power until the train was up to speed. A typical direct current (DC), traction diesel can generate full power virtually from a dead start, and can maintain full power at slow speeds for short periods of time. Diesels could also move a train much faster up a grade than steam. These characteristics gave diesels a distinct advantage moving heavy freight trains, especially in steeply graded territory. Railroads found that using diesels on mountain grades greatly simplified operations: Diesels permitted the elimination of many helper operations. Furthermore, diesels were capable of dynamic braking (using traction motors as generators). This was especially valuable for controlling heavy freight trains, further simplifying operations, and reducing brake shoe wear.

Diesels required far less maintenance than steam locomotives. In addition to labor-intensive fueling and watering procedures, a steam locomotive needed considerable daily maintenance: ashpans needed to be emptied; valves, valve gear, siderods, and other reciprocating parts needed regular lubrication and inspection; and steam boilers and fireboxes required routine inspection and mandatory maintenance—a boiler flaw could result in a catastrophic explosive disaster. Steam locomotives routinely required heavy shop work, while diesels do not. Diesel parts are typically made to a standard design, many of which are interchangeable between different models of the same manufacturer, while steam locomotive parts suffered from a gross lack of standardization. Both the degree and the difficulty of maintenance of steam engines compared to diesel had significant implications.

According to some studies, a typical steam locomotive would be available for service 45 percent of the time, compared to a diesel, which featured 90 to 95 percent availability. Diesels could be turned around and serviced much faster than steam. Greater availability meant a railroad needed fewer locomotives to cover its schedules. Since diesels could operate longer between servicing stops and required far less maintenance and very little heavy work, railroads could save money by drastically reducing shop forces, consolidating facilities, and streamlining maintenance programs.

There were numerous other advantages of dieselization, too. Employing diesels saved track and bridge maintenance, as diesels had lighter axle-loadings. Also, diesels, unlike steam, did not pound the track through dynamic augment.

Diesels were much cleaner than steam, a big selling point for early diesel switchers and a major advantage for passengers—no longer were riders (especially in non-air-conditioned coaches) subjected to long sooty rides that would soil their clothing and put cinders in their hair. Diesels were far less likely to emit hot embers that could cause trackside brush fires. Diesel maintenance facilities were potentially cleaner than conventional steam facilities (although some lines could rival the mess made by steam locomotives with poor diesel maintenance practice).

Diesels and Railroad Employment

The diesel promised to reduce railroad employment substantially, not just in the shop but on the road as well. Using multiple unit technology, one locomotive crew could operate any number of diesels. This had been one of the great advantages of electric locomotives as well. The diesel did not require a fireman, so hypothetically one man could run the train. Since diesels could operate faster, and greatly reduce transit time for some trains, railroads could potentially lengthen crew districts, thereby obtaining better manpower utilization.

In the steam era most crew districts had been set at about 100 miles—roughly the distance an average freight train could travel in eight hours. The prospect of reduced employment was embraced by railroad management, which hoped to reduce employment costs. But railroad workers threatened with the loss of their jobs fought for their job security. Diesel power therefore spawned decades of ill-will between management and labor.

Efforts to trim the work force were strongly resisted. Railroad unions had strong support, and some crafts were able to guarantee their positions, despite their perceived obsolescence or redundancy by management. The fireman survived on most railroads well into the 1960s, long after there had been any coal to shovel. But union efforts to keep additional crews on sets of multiple locomotives failed. The 100-mile run survived a generation after the last steam locomotives were retired, and it was not until the mid-1980s that railroads were finally able to benefit from significantly longer crew districts. Today 200- to 300-mile-long crew districts are not uncommon. But virtually all freight runs still have at least two men in the cab, primarily for safety reasons.

Railroads were able to trim employment in other ways. Diesels can haul more tonnage, allowing railroads to run fewer, but longer trains. When managed properly, this results in fewer crews to move the same tonnage over the road. In general, this principle works in the railroads' favor, although when taken to the extreme, it often backfires. Longer trains accelerate more slowly, and are far more prone to difficulties en route. They are more likely to stall ascending a grade, more likely to develop braking difficulties, and face a greater risk of derailment or mishap. This

does not discourage railroads from trying to run ever longer trains. In the steam era few freights exceeded 3,000 feet, and many were much shorter. Modern American railroads typically run trains more than 6,000 feet long and it's not unusual to find trains more than 10,000 feet on some lines—almost two miles long!

Disadvantages of Dieselization

The advantages of diesel operation were many, but there were disadvantages as well. The initial cost of dieselization was very high. New diesels cost two to three times more than steam engines based on horsepower—a fact steam manufacturers were quick to point out in their advertisements. Diesels required a higher level of workmanship than steam. Parts needed to be machined to closer tolerances, and there were many more parts per diesel locomotive than per steam locomotive.

While diesels required fewer shops, they required construction of all new facilities, which added substantially to the initial costs of converting. This at first restricted diesel operations to divisions that were equipped to maintain and supply this new form of motive power. Early during dieselization, many railroads would only operate diesels where they were needed the most, and only gradually expanded the diesels' operating territory. Diesels also required a whole new set of maintenance skills, forcing railroads to invest in retraining personnel and operational crews.

Diesels also enjoyed a shorter life span than steam. While steam required more daily maintenance, railroads expected to get 20 to 30 years out of most locomotives, and it was not unusual for some steam engines to operate for 40 years. Diesels had an average life span of just 15 years. After that they had to be completely rebuilt, or traded in. This shorter life span did have a positive effect in the more rapid introduction of new and more-efficient technology.

Resisting the Diesel

Railroaders had grown up around steam locomotives, and steam was deeply embedded in railroading culture. This was part nostalgia and sentimental attachment, but there was an economic component as well. Part of the railroads' economic livelihood involved hauling coal and supplying raw materials to the engine builders. Diesels resulted in fewer employees and the wholesale elimination of traditional shop crafts. Diesels also transferred motive power design tasks from the individual railroads to outside locomotive builders. Traditionally the railroad's motive power engineers had worked closely with locomotive manufacturers in producing new designs. Diesels, however, were generally not tailored to a railroad's specific needs. Thus age-old conventions of motive power requisition were dispensed with in favor of standardization. This was very hard for motive power chiefs to accept, especially because they had taken great pride in their fleets and in their design skills.

Railroads, in general, were notoriously slow to change, and many railroad executives and managers resisted the changes demanded by dieselization as long as they could, despite the cost advantages. The first serious interest in mainline dieselization dated to the mid-1920s, but it would be another 35 years before the changeover was complete.

Many railroads were closely linked to the coal industry. They often owned coal mines and relied on the shipment of coal as a large part of their freight revenue. While diesels offered lower operating costs, this advantage was less pertinent to roads with an abundant and cheap coal supply. Some lines did not want to risk offending their important coal customers. The staunchest supporters perpetuating steam power at the end were those lines with the closest links to the coal industry: the Pennsylvania Railroad, Chesapeake & Ohio, Duluth, Missabe & Iron Range, and of course, the Norfolk & Western—the last major American railroad to relinquish its steam fleet, which ran until 1960.

Opposite
On a sunny July 5, 1958, an A-B-A set of EMD F7s sits in front of the diesel shops at Pennsylvania's Enola Yard. Enola, situated on the west bank of the Susquehanna River opposite Harrisburg, was the western end of PRR's electrification and a traditional gathering point for steam, diesel, and electric locomotives. The F7 was the most common type of F-unit, and more than 3,600 were built for service on American railroads. *Richard Jay Solomon*

At Pica, Arizona, a few miles west of Seligman, a loaded coil steel train rolls west on the Santa Fe, catching the glint of the rising sun on January 23, 1994. A pair of Santa Fe's GE DASH8-40CWs lead two EMDs, including one of Santa Fe's many cowl locomotives. Santa Fe's Chicago to California mainline, now operated by Burlington Northern Santa Fe, is one of the busiest freight lines in the West.

1

ELECTRICS

IN THE UNITED STATES the development of the diesel-electric locomotive was integrally linked with the development and application of steam railroad electrification. Electric railroad technology enabled the practical application of the diesel engine on American rails, and many of the benefits of railroad electrification are also provided by diesels. To better understand the role of the diesel-electric locomotive and the conditions that allowed it to swiftly become the primary type of motive power in America, after years of relative obscurity, it is important to understand the history and development of railroad electrification and electric locomotives.

Numerous novel experiments in electric railway propulsion had been undertaken during the mid-nineteenth century, but did not result in a sufficiently refined technology for widespread application. By the 1880s electrical technology had entered a new era. The development of practical electrical generation and distribution made railway applications possible.

Thomas Edison, one of the great pioneers and promoters of electrical technology (and founder of the General Electric Company), demonstrated small electric locomotives in the early 1880s. But Edison wanted to promote electricity itself, not electrical machines. That opportunity was seized by Frank Julian Sprague, a talented inventor and one-time employee of Edison.

Sprague became one of the foremost promoters and developers of electric railway technology. In 1885, he electrified a short portion of the Manhattan Railway, a steam-powered, elevated rapid transit line in New York City. The experiment met with limited success, but failed to generate serious interest in further electrification of the elevated lines at that time. Two years later, following experiments with battery-powered street cars in several cities, Sprague set an important electric railway precedent in Virginia by electrifying the Richmond Union Passenger Railway. In 1888 this operation featured 40 electric street cars operating over 12 miles of track. Prior to this development, most street railways were operated with horse-drawn cars. In 1873, the cable-powered street railway was introduced in San Francisco, and by the 1880s there were numerous successful cable car systems in American cities. Another method of street railway propulsion was steam-dummies—small, low-powered, reciprocating steam locomotives disguised to look like street cars.

In 1934, PRR hired famed industrial designer Raymond Loewy to improve the appearance of its new electric locomotive. While the locomotive already had a distinctive streamlined shape, Loewy suggested welding the carbody, and he cleaned up many design elements and added the famous "Cat's whiskers" striping. The GG1 became one of the most recognizable locomotives in the United States and typified the whole streamlined Art Deco era. On May 10, 1959, a GG1 races through Monmouth Junction, New Jersey. *Richard Jay Solomon*

In the 1950s the development of ignitron rectifier technology resulted in a new breed of electrics, and the Virginian Railway ordered a small fleet of 3,300 horsepower rectifier freight motors from GE. After N&W took over, then discontinued, Virginian's electric operations in 1962, New Haven bought the rectifiers to re-electrify its New York freight services, which had been temporarily converted to diesel. In May 1964 a pair of EF-4s bring a long freight across the Hell Gate bridge in New York City, only a few months after they entered service. *Richard Jay Solomon*

Sprague's electric street railway was a spectacular success. Cities invested hundreds of millions of dollars in the application of the new technology and in less than a decade there were more than 850 different electric railway companies operating roughly 9,000 miles of track in the United States. In addition to urban street railways, a new breed of railway had emerged—the interurban line. The interurban was usually built to much lower standards than conventional steam railways. Most lines were comparatively short, often operating in streets or along the side of the road, usually connecting small towns and cities. The interurbans often competed directly with steam railways, which they could do because of lower operating expenses from electric power.

Street railway and interurban cars were substantially lighter, and the conditions for operation were usually less demanding than those of steam railways. As a result, it was several years before Frank Sprague's ideas were applied to a serious steam railroad application. But by the early 1890s, the concept of electrified railroading had taken hold, and it was just a matter of time for the technology to be perfected.

THE B&O EMBRACES ELECTRICITY

In the late 1880s, Baltimore & Ohio was looking to improve its route through Baltimore by constructing a new belt line directly through a tunnel downtown, but smoke pollution concerns produced considerable opposition. Baltimore & Ohio officials were unable to pacify objections to their plan until they announced a novel solution to the smoke problem in the early 1890s, one that had never been tried before: electrification.

Baltimore & Ohio selected General Electric to supply electrical support and locomotives. The only effective railway electrification system at that time was the basic direct current system used by street railways and interurbans, so GE developed a 600-volt DC arrangement, using a peculiar system of overhead electric delivery. The electrified section was roughly 3 miles long. The electrics were designed to couple to the front of the steam locomotive and haul the whole train through the tunnel, steam locomotive and all.

It is fitting that America's pioneering steam-powered common carrier, and one of the first American railroads to use domestically built steam locomotives as opposed to imported locomotives from England, was also the first line to embrace mainline electrification. While the Baltimore Belt Line electrification was very short, it represented the first serious application of mainline electrification in the world, and was in service nearly a decade before other major electrification systems in the United States.

WHY ELECTRIFY?

While the Baltimore & Ohio was the only steam railroad to adopt a regular mainline electrification as early as 1895, it was not the only railroad to experiment with the

In a rare vintage photograph, New York Central T-motor 3405 (later rebuilt and reclassed as an "S-motor") poses with a consist of wooden passenger cars in front of the old Grand Central Station train shed at 42nd Street in New York City. Judging by the crowds, this was the inauguration of electric service in 1906. *Richard Jay Solomon collection*

Pennsylvania Railroad GG1 electric 4936 leads an eastbound train across a rural grade crossing east of Lancaster, in Pennsylvania Dutch country. The PRR was one of the few American lines to embrace large-scale mainline electrification. *Richard Jay Solomon*

technology. That year both the Pennsylvania and the New Haven Railroads electrified short branchlines, efforts that would lead to further experimentation and ultimately extensive mainline electrifications. Initially both railroads tried DC overhead trolley wire, the standard of the period, but later they also experimented with DC third-rail systems. By 1901 New Haven had electrified several branches in Massachusetts, Rhode Island, and Connecticut, and the Pennsylvania Railroad electrified branches in New Jersey, Pennsylvania, and its Long Island Rail Road subsidiary.

Many railroads had an interest in electrification and carefully monitored the progress of railroads that risked capital to experiment with this new mode of powering trains. For every railroad that played "wait and see," a question stuck in the minds of management: Why consider abandoning the steam locomotive, which had successfully satisfied the railroads' motive power needs for generations? Since the first locomotives entered the scene in the early part of the nineteenth century, steam locomotive design had consistently improved, gradually producing better and more-efficient designs.

Electrification offered many advantages that even the finest, most technologically advanced steam locomotives could not match, and by the early twentieth century, many of these advantages were understood. Electrified operations were substantially cleaner than steam. Power plants could be located away from urban centers, eliminating the need for smoke-belching locomotives operating within built-up areas. By the 1890s, the great volume of rail traffic in the center of many American cities had posed a serious pollution problem, and the ability to minimize smoke was hailed as a great advantage. It also allowed for cleaner passenger trains, removing the soot and ash that often enveloped a steam locomotive. In an era when electric streetcar companies and interurbans were rapidly eroding steam railroads' local passenger base, this was an important consideration.

Electrically operated locomotives and cars also had a functional advantage over steam. They were significantly more powerful, providing greater starting tractive effort and higher horsepower than steam. This allowed a single train crew to do more work, and it streamlined operations. Since an electric train could start and get up to speed much faster than a comparable passenger train, electric service was better suited for suburban commuter runs, where on-time operation was important, and trains often made frequent stops. By using electric power, a railroad could dramatically increase mainline

capacity without adding tracks. Service availability was another issue: steam locomotives required elaborate fueling, watering, and running maintenance procedures relating to the firebox and boiler; electrics, by contrast, were basically ready to head out on the next run as soon as they arrived at the terminal. As a result electrification greatly improved terminal capacity and terminal costs. Another cost-saving feature: the greater availability and improved pulling power of electrics dramatically reduced the number of locomotives required for a given service.

In 1897, Frank Sprague's development of electric-pneumatic multiple-unit operation gave added incentive to electrification. Multiple-unit operation enabled a single operator to control a number of electric cars (known as Multiple Units or MUs) or locomotives from a single control position. Steam locomotives required a locomotive engineer for each locomotive, and this dramatically increased labor costs when multiple locomotives were required on a single train. It was not uncommon for a heavy, long-distance passenger train to run doubleheaded, and freight trains might use as many as a half-dozen locomotives or more to surmount a particularly steep grade. MU capability was therefore particularly attractive for steep mountainous operations, where multiple steam locomotives were routinely used to move heavy trains. In passenger operations, electrically powered multiple-unit passenger cars dispensed with the need for locomotives entirely, allowing for improved turnaround time at stub-end terminals without turning.

AC versus DC

The two primary American suppliers of electrical equipment were General Electric and Westinghouse. These

In the circle at the left is one of the electric locomotives that will replace the steam engines.

10 locomotives will
take the place of 25

Electric locomotives draw long trains 650 miles over the Rocky Mountains on the Chicago, Milwaukee and St. Paul. Eventually most of the railroads in America will be electrified—engineers estimate that this will save more than a hundred million tons of coal a year.

The General Electric Company is electrifying the Mexican Railway between Orizaba and Esperanza. On the first section—with many curves and heavy grades—10 *electric* locomotives will take the place of 25 *steam* locomotives.

Economies resulting from electrification will repay the cost of the improvement within five or six years.

GENERAL ELECTRIC

An optimistic General Electric ad from the mid-1920s boasts that ". . . most of the railroads in America will be electrified." In essence they were correct, but railroads chose diesel-electrics over straight electric operation. *Author collection*

A pair of boxcab electrics switches Milwaukee's Harlowton, Montana, yard as a pair of GE "Little Joe" electrics pass with an eastbound freight on an adjacent track. These locomotives, built in 1948, were originally destined for Russia, but were instead sold domestically to Milwaukee and the South Shore as a result of Cold War politics, and nicknamed for Joe Stalin. Milwaukee's Pacific Extension electrification was the longest in the United States. *Mel Patrick*

The Oneonta & Mohawk Valley, which operated in rural upstate New York at the turn of the century, was a typical American interurban electric railway. Interurbans were the first serious competition to the steam railways. Electric cars such as this one were the precursor to gas-electric cars, which ultimately resulted in the development of the first diesel-electric locomotives.
Richard Jay Solomon collection

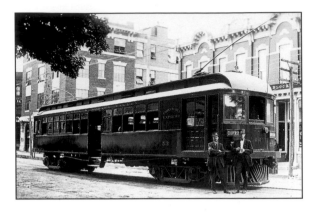

Opposite
On September 11, 1958, a New York Central T-2b electric races northward at 153rd Street in The Bronx. Although New York Central considered electrifying its extremely heavily traveled lines into Grand Central as early as 1899, a tragic wreck in the smoke-filled Park Avenue Tunnel in 1902 forced the issue. Grand Central Terminal no longer serves long-distance trains, and today the majority of Metro North's suburban trains are electric multiple units. *Richard Jay Solomon*

companies were fierce competitors embracing differing electrical engineering philosophies. General Electric, Edison's company, promoted DC systems, while Westinghouse, founded by George Westinghouse, a man best known for the development of the first successful air brake, promoted alternating current (AC). AC was eventually selected as the most appropriate system for most large-scale power grids, but at the turn of the century DC was still preferred for electric railway purposes, and nearly all the electrified street railways and interurbans used direct current (though there were a few exceptions). The debate over DC and AC systems for heavy railway applications would continue well into the twentieth century, as both systems had distinct advantages and disadvantages. In 1896, GE and Westinghouse exchanged patents allowing both companies to market either technology. Yet both continued to promote their own inventions. Joining up with the two largest locomotive manufacturers in the United States, in 1895, Baldwin and Westinghouse entered a partnership to market mainline electrification, and GE and Alco later formed a similar arrangement. These partnerships would survive well into the diesel era.

AC and DC power each presented benefits and drawbacks. DC transmission systems were simpler than AC, and DC motors were initially more efficient and easier to control for railway applications than AC motors. However, DC is not an efficient system for long-distance transmission and requires frequent, expensive substations to maintain adequate power levels. AC was much better suited to large-scale electrification schemes, as it could be transmitted more efficiently over long distances. AC required far fewer substations, resulting in lower costs for a large system.

WHEEL ARRANGEMENTS

In America, the Whyte system, which counts wheels and organizes them into three basic groups (leading, driving, and trailing), is used for steam locomotives. Another different system is applied to diesels and electrics: axles were counted instead of wheels, grouping them by truck arrangement (axles held together in a swiveling frame). Powered axles are identified by letter: A for one axle, B for two axles, and so on, while unpowered axles are identified by number: either one or 2. Typical modern wheel arrangements accounting for the vast majority of diesel electric locomotives in use today are B-B and C-C. Passenger locomotives, such as EMD's E-units, used A1A trucks with an unpowered center axle. A few specialized locomotives such as EMD's dual mode FL9 use a B-A1A arrangement. Straight electrics often employed more-complicated wheel arrangements involving articulated sections designated with a + sign. For example, Pennsylvania Railroad's GG1 electrics featured a 2-C+C-2 arrangement. In the 1960s, several builders produced eight-axle diesels, some of these models used a D-D arrangement (two four-axle trucks), others a B-B+B-B setup (four groups of two-axle trucks.)

Above: In 1938, New Haven ordered six bidirectional streamlined passenger electrics from General Electric; they weighed 216 tons and delivered 3,600 horsepower. *Below right:* In July 1958, a 20-year-old EP-4 electric rolls eastbound through Stamford, Connecticut, beneath New Haven's 1905–1907 vintage triangular catenary, erected for the railroad's pioneering 11,000-volt AC mainline electrification. *Richard Jay Solomon*

Opposite
In 1953, New York Central dieselized its Cleveland Union Terminal electrification and transferred its big CUT electrics to New York. In the early 1960s an ex-CUT P-motor leads part of Central's "Great Steel Fleet"—a common nickname for New York Central's comprehensive passenger service—south of Harmon, New York. *Richard Jay Solomon*

However AC was significantly more complex—AC motors were larger and required more complex control equipment. The heated argument among railway engineers at the turn of the century over DC vs. AC power resumed in the 1990s with the introduction of practical AC traction for diesel-electric locomotives. While the technology evolves and gets more complex, the basic principles of each system remain the same.

New York City Forces the Issue

By 1900, the extremely high volume of passenger traffic into New York City resulted in several of the regional commuter railroads seriously considering electrification as a way of improving capacity, overcoming serious air quality problems, and allowing for the construction of long tunnels to improve traffic flow and access.

The Long Island Rail Road, which the Pennsylvania Railroad (PRR) acquired control of in the 1890s, struggled to keep its mainline fluid, and was operating steam-powered trains to its East River ferry terminals opposite Manhattan at two- and three-minute headways during rush hours. Long Island was investigating the construction of tunnels that would bring its trains directly into Manhattan. The operation of long tunnels would have been prohibitively dangerous with steam locomotives, especially considering the volume of traffic. Long Island's parent, the Pennsylvania, had also been

contemplating building either a bridge or tunnels across the Hudson River for direct access to Manhattan Island.

Perhaps the most pressing congestion problems were experienced by the two major railroads that were already operating directly into Manhattan, the New York Central and New York New Haven & Hartford (New Haven). These railroads both terminated at the famous Grand Central Station in the middle of Manhattan at 42nd Street. Congestion on the approaches along Park Avenue had reached a breaking point. The greatest problem lay in the 2-mile-long, four-track Park Avenue Tunnel, where dense smoke often obscured signals, making operations hazardous and the air difficult to breathe. In 1899, New York Central began studying electrification as way of relieving congestion and eliminating its smoke problem. By 1902, plans for a greatly expanded new Grand Central Terminal were under way. Yet it wasn't just the hypothetical savings and anticipated capacity relief that convinced New York Central to electrify.

On the morning of January 8, 1902, tragedy struck. An inbound New York Central train overran a signal in the smoke-filled Park Avenue Tunnel and collided with a stopped New Haven suburban train. When the dust settled, 15 passengers were dead and many more injured. While this sort of accident was not particularly unusual for the period (the famed Casey Jones was killed in a similar rear-end collision), the public outrage following the Park Avenue disaster had serious long-term effects on the motive power used in New York City. Soon after the crash, New York passed strict legislation requiring railroads to eliminate steam locomotive operation within the city limits, not just into Grand Central, but on all railroads serving New York. In the short term, this played an important role in the development and application of heavy railroad electrification in the United States. In the longer term it directly resulted in the first commercially successful diesel-electrics, and other important early diesel research, because of the need to eliminate steam switchers from New York City railroad yards.

New York Central set up the Electric Traction Commission to study electrification alternatives. This body included many of the top authorities in the field, including electric railway pioneer Frank Sprague. Based on the commission's recommendations, experience learned from B&O's electrification, and the electrification of the New

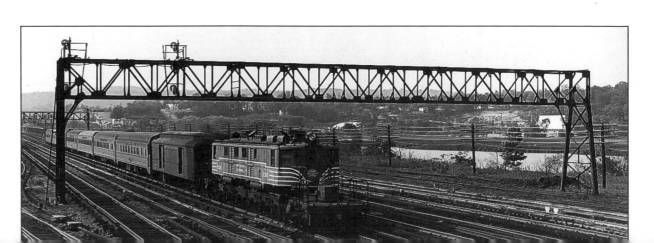

York, Brooklyn, and Chicago elevated railways, New York Central chose a 600-volt DC system using an underrunning outside third rail (meaning the third rail shoe made contact with the underside of the third rail, as opposed to the more common overrunning third rail where the shoe ran on the top of the rail). General Electric was chosen to provide electrical gear and locomotives.

Initially New York Central only electrified Grand Central Terminal trackage and short sections of its Hudson and Harlem lines, bringing the electrification to the edge of urban development. Eventually the electrification was extended all the way to Croton-on-Hudson (today referred to as Croton Harmon) on the Hudson River Line (1913), and to North White Plains on the Harlem Line (1910). More electrification was installed in the 1920s as the railroad purged its remaining steam power from New York City.

The New Haven also electrified its lines to New York City, but chose an overhead 11,000-volt AC system instead of New York Central's DC third rail (with dual AC/DC equipment for operation into Grand Central). The Pennsylvania Railroad electrified its new Manhattan terminal and tunnels using an underrunning DC third rail system identical to the Long Island's. Later, PRR electrified its Philadelphia suburban lines with an overhead system similar to New Haven's. Ultimately this AC system would become the most extensive mainline electrification in the United States, from New York to Washington mainline, and west to Harrisburg, with a multitude of PRR suburban and secondary lines for both freight and passenger service.

By 1925, a number of American railroads had electrified sections, commuter lines, city terminals, and numerous long tunnels where smoke problems had proved difficult. However, there were only a few long sections of main line electrification beyond Pennsylvania's lines, with each railroad specifying different AC or DC voltages. As a result, there were few industry standards. One of the most interesting and most extensive projects was Milwaukee Road's Pacific Extension electrification. Two long but disconnected segments represented more than 600 miles of heavy mountain mainline electrification at 3,000-volts DC.

While many mainline U.S. railroads seriously investigated the numerous benefits of heavy electrification, the enormous costs involved precluded its adoption on a widespread scale. Overseas, different economic conditions prevailed, and railways in Europe and Japan benefited from widespread electrification. Ultimately, American lines chose diesel-electrics instead, in effect a form of electrification. Through dieselization, U.S. railroads enjoyed many of the benefits of electrification without the cost of building substations and overhead wires or third rails. The successful diesel-electric not only doomed the once-ubiquitous steam locomotive, but also quelled interest in most proposed electrification projects.

New York Central's third-rail DC electrification was one of the first large-scale electric operations in the United States. On June 27, 1959, a T2b electric rolls north through Dobbs Ferry, New York, on the Hudson River Line. New York Central's T-motors were the preferred mainline electrics for four decades. *Richard Jay Solomon*

Wearing a Northeast Direct paint scheme, Amtrak AEM-7 electric No. 940 leads a northbound train across the former Pennsylvania Railroad Susquehanna River Bridge at Perryville, Maryland, in November 1997. This electric is a Swedish design, built by EMD for Amtrak under license from Allmänna Svenska Elektriska Aktiebolaget. Amtrak's electrified territory runs from Washington Union Station to New Haven, Connecticut (with an extension of the wires under construction to Boston), and from Philadelphia west to Harrisburg.

2

Railcars, Boxcabs, and Streamliners

THE EARLY TWENTIETH CENTURY saw great innovation and investment in railroad technology. The traditional steam railroads, which had been the dominant transportation force in the nineteenth century, were now facing increasing threats of competition, first from lightly built electric railways, then more seriously from highway transport, and later airplanes. As the railroads searched for a more efficient and economical way to run trains, another concern forced them to consider new technology: smoke pollution. Cities were demanding that railways develop cleaner motive power. Electrically powered trains solved part of the problem in a few cities, but the cost of heavy railroad electrification was prohibitively expensive for most lines. Ultimately hybrid internal combustion-electric technology emerged as the most effective and efficient way to power trains and was rapidly developed in the 1920s and 1930s. By the 1960s this hybrid had supplanted traditional steam power.

Early Railcars

Self-propelled railcars had been employed since the early days of railroading as a way of reducing costs on lightly traveled lines. Many early railcars were powered by small

steam engines; others used a variety of novel—and mostly unsuccessful—methods of propulsion. In 1890 William Patton built a gasoline-electric-powered railcar using a small, 10-horsepower Van Duzen engine. This is believed to be the first such application of this technology to a railway vehicle. Patton built more gasoline-electric railcars, but ended their production in 1893. Later, he built a few gasoline-electric locomotives, but his ideas did not have an immediate impact on the development of more-effective technology. Although Patton was unsuccessful, his concepts later achieved considerable success, and gasoline-powered railcars became a popular solution for reducing the cost of branchline operations.

McKeen Railcars

Following the turn of the century, Union Pacific, like many railways, was looking for ways to cut costs on its branchline and secondary passenger services. In 1904, Edward Henry Harriman, who controlled both Union Pacific (UP) and Southern Pacific (SP), urged UP's motive power chief, William J. McKeen, to develop a practical railcar suitable for passenger service on Harriman's railroads. At Harriman's urging, McKeen and UP's engineers designed a prototype railcar

The Pennsylvania Railroad was among the last railroads to regularly use traditional railcars, often described as "Doodlebugs." On a hazy June 8, 1958, Pennsylvania Railroad doodlebug No. 4669 pauses a Monmouth Junction, New Jersey. The car was built by Brill as a gas-electric, powered by a Brill-WH 660 engine, but during World War II it was repowered with a Hamilton 425 horsepower diesel engine. *Richard Jay Solomon*

that embraced wind-resistance principles developed through the Berlin-Zossen high-speed propulsion tests in Germany and similar experiments conducted in St. Louis by the Electric Railway Test Commission in 1904. Wind resistance increases as a vehicle moves faster; although this resistance is negligible at slow speeds, it has a demonstrably negative effect on performance and efficiency at higher speeds.

McKeen's first "Windsplitter" car, No. M-1, was constructed at Union Pacific's Omaha Shops in March 1905 and featured a knife-edge front end and a rounded rear to reduce wind resistance. The car was 31 feet long and rode on a single two-axle truck with 42-inch wheels. It was powered by an 8x10-inch vertical six-cylinder Riotte gasoline engine that developed 100 horsepower. A Standard Motor Works mechanical transmission engaged the drive axle using a chain drive. Harriman was anxious to try the car in Portland, Oregon, where anti-smoke regulations, similar to those passed in New York City, were threatening to hamper railroad operations. After brief tests in Omaha and Salt Lake City, the car went to Portland. While it did not perform as well as expected, McKeen followed with another prototype. This one was 55 feet long and featured two trucks with a seating capacity for 57 passengers.

McKeen refined his design and additional cars followed the early prototypes, embodying characteristic McKeen design qualities. The typical McKeen car was 70 feet long, used an all-steel body with McKeen's knife-edge front and rounded rear, and featured rows of distinctive porthole windows and a rounded tapered roof. The cars typically weighed between 34 and 40 tons, and used a 200-horsepower gasoline engine of McKeen's design. (McKeen had adapted a marine engine design for use on his cars in 1906.) Quite advanced aesthetically for its time, the Windsplitter was unlikely to be mistaken for anything else on the rails, and except for the cowcatcher pilot constructed of steel bars, it displayed a remarkably futuristic appearance.

In 1908, Harriman provided McKeen with resources to set up the McKeen Railcar Company, and McKeen resigned his position at UP to build railcars full time. His primary customers were UP and SP, with SP owning the largest fleet of McKeen railcars. McKeen's business boomed for a few years. He sold most of his cars between 1909 and 1912, then his business dropped off. The cars suffered from reliability problems that greatly affected future sales. The principal flaw was poor engine placement and the mechanical transmission. Locating the engine on the power truck subjected it to jarring,

Opposite
The gas-electric was designed to reduce operating costs on rural branch lines. The East Broad Top was a coal-hauling narrow gauge line in central Pennsylvania, which ordered a gas-electric kit from J.G. Brill in 1926, assembling the car in its company shops at Orbisonia, Pennsylvania. It is believed to be the only 3-foot gauge gas-electric built in America. Today it survives as the only remaining gas-electric car in its original form.

damaging forces as the car rolled along, a problem magnified because the cars were often assigned to lightweight branchlines with poor track conditions. The transmission was inappropriate for the car's design, and McKeen cars were notorious for rough starts and burned-out clutches. The advent of World War I had a disastrous effect on McKeen's business. He sold very few cars after 1914. His company built its last car in 1917, and in 1920 Union Pacific absorbed McKeen's remaining assets.

Despite their flaws, a few McKeen cars operated into the 1930s, and McKeen lived until 1946, having profited quite nicely from UP's buyout. McKeen's influence on later development had a far profounder effect on the industry than his railcars did. Edward G. Budd was among McKeen's engineers responsible for the cars' design. He later founded the Budd Company, which built the Burlington's famous *Zephyr* (discussed on page 45), became a principal supplier of railway passenger cars, and later developed the most successful railcar in America: the rail-diesel-car (RDC), popularly known as the "Budd-car." Budd admitted in later years that his later designs profited from mistakes made on the McKeen car.

General Electric

General Electric was one of the first companies in the United States to manufacture gas-electric railcars, and it viewed this business as a logical complement to both its street and interurban electric railway business and its heavy railway electrification plans. The gas-electric railcar represented a very small portion of GE's income, yet GE's involvement in the gas-electric industry had a profound long-term impact on the development of the American diesel locomotive, helping to shape diesel locomotive technology in its infancy.

General Electric closely followed the development of gas-electric cars in England, where they had been in regular

Union Pacific McKeen Windsplitter M-18 rolls across the South Platte River bridge in Denver, Colorado, on May 23, 1931. While the McKeen car was not especially successful, it inspired more-significant developments in internal combustion propulsion.
Otto Perry, Denver Public Library Western History Department

Although it was not the first diesel-electric built in the United States, Central Railroad of New Jersey No. 1000, built by Alco-GE-IR in 1925, is heralded as the first commercially successful diesel-electric locomotive in America. It spent most of its career working CNJ's isolated yard at 138th Street in The Bronx, New York. It is now proudly displayed at the Baltimore & Ohio Railroad Museum in Baltimore.

use since the turn of the century. In 1904 (the same year that GE built the New York Central's prototype electric locomotive for the Grand Central Terminal electrification), it experimented with a wooden Barney & Smith combine-coach provided by the Delaware & Hudson and a Wolseley gasoline engine imported from England. Learning from these early trials, GE went on to develop its own gasoline engine line.

Beginning in 1906, GE began selling commercial gas-electric railcars and during the next eight years built 88. Among GE's railcar customers was the newly formed Minneapolis, St. Paul, Rochester & Dubuque Electric Traction Company, an interurban railway better known as the Dan Patch Line. While it was similar to many interurban lines operating all over the United States, it differed from most "electric" railways in that it used gas-electric technology instead of an overhead trolley wire or third rail. The growing motive power needs of the Dan Patch Lines outpaced the self-propelled gas-electric, so General Electric expanded the concept by building a small boxcab gas-electric locomotive.

On a car body constructed by the Wason Car Company of Springfield, Massachusetts—one of GE's principal suppliers for its gas-electric car bodies—GE installed two eight-cylinder, 8x10-inch V-8 engines rated at 175 horsepower each. The locomotive was 36 feet, 4 inches long, weighed 57 tons, and rode on a pair of two-axle trucks, giving it a B-B wheel arrangement typical of interurban straight electrics of the period. While not the very first gasoline-electric locomotive (Patton had constructed some in the 1890s), the Dan Patch No. 100 is generally considered as the first commercially successful internal combustion-electric locomotive in the United States. General Electric constructed a similar locomotive, weighing just 45 tons, for its own test purposes about the same time. This engine was later to sold to the Jay Street Connecting Railroad, a waterfront switching line in Brooklyn, New York. The success of the Dan Patch 100 prompted the railway to order from GE three slightly larger locomotives—41 feet, 4 inches long, weighing 60 tons—delivered by 1915. A year later, the Dan Patch Lines became the Minneapolis, Northfield & Southern. Its gas-electric locomotives had a roughly 30-year career. Today the Dan Patch 100 is preserved in Minneapolis.

Despite its relative success in the railcar business and its pioneering venture into internal-combustion traction, GE effectively exited the gas-electric railcar market in 1914, although it continued to produce a handful of gas-electrics until 1917.

Rudolf Diesel's Engine

In the 1890s, German inventor Rudolf Diesel perfected the world's first successful internal-combustion, compression-ignition engine. When a gas is compressed, its temperature rises; the greater the compression, the higher the heat. Diesel's engine used the heated gases generated by compression to ignite fuel injected into the cylinder at the appropriate moment for combustion (in contrast to a typical gasoline engine, which requires a spark plug for ignition). Diesel's engine was an extraordinarily effective design that achieved thermal efficiency roughly four times greater than typical steam engines of the period. (Thermal efficiency is a measure of how well an engine converts its fuel to the work delivered.)

Initially, diesel engines were built for stationary purposes, but Diesel was more than just a clever engineer, he was a remarkable visionary. He imagined that his engine might be used to replace the steam locomotive in railway service. He spent the remainder of his life refining his engine and promoting its potential. Diesel made several tours of the United States and influenced a number of top railway officials toward the possibilities of diesel power. Sadly, Diesel died mysteriously in a suspicious boating accident in 1913, just a few years before the first commercial diesel locomotives made their debut on the American market. Shortly before he died, he witnessed the first application of his railway engine on a Swiss-built diesel-mechanical prototype.

The First American Diesel Locomotives

In the early years, the main advantage of diesel over other internal combustion designs was its much lower fuel cost. Diesels could burn a low-grade petroleum distillate that cost only half the price of gasoline.

In 1917, General Electric pioneered another technological development by constructing an experimental diesel-electric locomotive based on its earlier gas-electric locomotive designs. It used a GM50 engine, a V-8 diesel engine of GE's own design. It was similar to GE's gasoline engines and, according to railroading author John Kirkland, it employed concepts adopted from German Junkers engines designed for aircraft application. It produced 225 horsepower, 50 more than GE's gasoline engine, and weighed almost 7 tons. In 1918, GE built several diesel-electrics, but all were commercial failures. One was delivered to the Jay Street Connecting Railroad, designated No. 4, and joined the earlier GE gas-electric, No. 3. Two others were built, one for the City of Baltimore, the other for the U.S. Army. None of the diesels performed well and all had very short careers. At this time GE decided to exit the engine business. Though its early efforts failed to interest the railroads or to produce a practical, commercially viable diesel-electric locomotive, it prompted additional R&D.

General Electric and engine producer Ingersoll Rand (IR) joined forces in 1923 to build an experimental diesel-electric locomotive using GE electrical and mechanical components and IR's successful diesel engine, a 10x12-inch (bore x stroke), six-cylinder engine that operated at 550 rpm and generated 300 horsepower. The locomotive, designated No. 8835 (its construction number), first moved under its own power at Phillipsburg, Pennsylvania, on December 17,

1923, and was publicly demonstrated two months later. In June 1924, the locomotive began an extensive tour and was tested by 13 different railway companies, including the Baltimore & Ohio, Central Railroad of New Jersey, Lackawanna, Long Island Rail Road, New Haven, and New York Central.

Development of this diesel prototype coincided with the Kaufman Act legislation in New York City that expanded on earlier laws banning all steam locomotives within New York City by 1926. While most passenger operations had been electrified under the early law, many freight and switching operations remained steam powered, including those in small yards along the waterfront. The worst offender was New York Central's West Side Freight line in Manhattan, particularly the lower end below 33rd Street, where the tracks ran on 11th Avenue and on other streets to reach customers.

Unlike New York Central, most New York area railroads were not afforded direct land access to the city. Instead they served New York via car float and barges, reaching small isolated yards along its rivers and bays. It was not economically viable to electrify most of these small yards, so the diesel switcher provided the perfect solution to comply with the Kaufman Act. While amendments postponed the 1926 deadline, the Kaufman Act, like the legislation that preceded it, eventually forced railroads to seek alternative power and effectively created the emergent market for diesel-electric switchers.

Diesels at What Cost?

In these early years of diesel development, there was no perceived cost advantage of diesel operation over steam. The extremely high compression ratio required to obtain fuel combustion required exceptionally sturdy, and therefore very heavy, engine components. Diesel engines were typically made of thick cast iron and were large, ponderous machines. It was difficult to make one small enough to fit inside a locomotive body, and early diesels had very poor weight-to-horsepower ratios.

Despite these drawbacks, several companies saw the promise of diesel technology. Based on the success of the 8835 experimental, GE, Ingersoll Rand, and Alco entered a consortium to construct diesel-electric switching locomotives. Under this arrangement, Alco supplied mechanical gear—in the same fashion it had for many GE straight elec-

Inside the boxcab is the machinery that makes the locomotive work. Central Railroad of New Jersey No. 1000 was powered by a six-cylinder 10x12-inch (bore and stroke) Ingersoll-Rand diesel engine that generated 300 horsepower working at 550 rpm. This enormous, heavy engine was ponderously slow compared to later diesel engines that use alloyed steel blocks and operate as fast as 950 rpm.

The Alco-GE-IR consortium was the first to successfully market diesel-electric locomotives in the United States. The principal markets for these early diesels were isolated switching operations in New York City, and the first commercially built locomotive was Central Railroad of New Jersey No. 1000, which worked in The Bronx. The Lackawanna bought two Alco-GE-IR 300-ton boxcabs, one of which was lettered Harlem Transfer No. 2. It was assigned to Lackawanna's car float terminal at 132nd street, just a few blocks from the CNJ terminal, where it was photographed on February 8, 1959. *Richard Jay Solomon*

tric locomotives; GE provided electrical components; and Ingersoll Rand provided the diesel engine and was responsible for marketing. The diesel-electric was viewed as a specialty outgrowth of the electric locomotive business and not viewed as a serious competitor to steam power. Between 1925 and 1928, the Alco-GE-IR consortium built a number of boxcab diesel-electrics, primarily for switching in Eastern cities, especially New York. The consortium offered two models: a 60-ton, 300-horsepower locomotive similar to demonstrator 8835, although with cabs at both ends; and a dual engine, 100-ton locomotive that generated 600 horsepower.

Central Railroad of New Jersey took delivery of the first commercial locomotive, a 300-horsepower boxcab, No. 1000. This pioneering locomotive, widely regarded as the first successful diesel-electric built in the United States, was assigned to CNJ's isolated waterfront terminal in The Bronx, New York. Unlike earlier diesels, No. 1000 enjoyed a long, productive career, running longer than 30 years in the service for which it was built. It was finally retired in 1957, and sent to the Baltimore & Ohio Railroad Museum

in Baltimore. Alco-GE-IR built 33 locomotives between 1925 and 1928. After Alco left the consortium in 1928, GE-IR continued to manufacture diesels for a few more years.

New York Central's Early Diesel Interest

The Kaufman Act forced New York Central to investigate alternative means to operate its vast New York City freight operations. In the 1920s New York City was the largest single market on New York Central and it operated dozens of through freights to the New York area every day. Many of these either terminated in The Bronx, or continued down Central's busy double-track West Side Line and terminated in one of several yards on Manhattan Island. New York Central also needed a way of powering trains on its lightly traveled Putnam Division, which terminated in New York City but did not enjoy the traffic density that had afforded the electrification of the Central's Harlem and Hudson Lines.

Most of the West Side Line was electrified with third rail in conjunction with a massive grade separation program

Reading Company 99 was a 300-horsepower Alco-GE-IR diesel switcher built to the same specifications as Central Railroad of New Jersey 1000. It is seen working street trackage in Philadelphia on June 24, 1947. It has all the trappings of a steam-era locomotive, including large headlight, heavy brass bell, and pole pockets on the pilot, used for positioning freight cars with a wooden pole. *J.R. Quinn collection*

New York Central tri-power switcher No. 561 switches in Chicago on August 10, 1939. New York Central operated the first large fleet of diesel-powered locomotives in order to comply with strict air pollution laws in New York City and Chicago. *Otto Perry, Denver Public Library Western History Department*

to get the tracks off the city streets. A short portion of the Putnam Division to Yonkers and freight branch in The Bronx was also electrified in the late 1920s. This did not solve the entire smoke pollution problem, however, and New York Central was still faced with a complicated switching scenario. While the West Side trunk was electrified, the numerous spurs and sidings serving its customers were not; furthermore, the new West Side elevated structure passed directly through warehouses and businesses, some of which had spurs that went into their buildings, such as Bell Labs. Smoke belching locomotives of any kind, steam or diesel, could not operate in these confined areas.

To solve Central's switching quandary, GE and Alco developed a tri-power locomotive that fulfilled the railroad's demands. It could operate as a straight third-rail electric, as a battery-electric from onboard storage batteries, or as a battery-electric/diesel-electric, drawing power from both batteries and the onboard diesel engine. The diesel engine would charge the batteries, but the third-rail connection could not. After testing a prototype tri-power

locomotive in February 1928 that used a center-cab configuration, New York Central ordered a fleet of tri-power locomotives using a more typical boxcab configuration. While most tri-power locomotives worked in the New York terminal area, some were assigned to Chicago, Detroit, and Boston. (Another locomotive, built to New York Central specs, was delivered to the Rock Island for switching at LaSalle Street Station in Chicago.)

New York Central ordered both experimental road freight and passenger boxcab diesel-electric locomotives. Boxcab No. 1550 was completed by Alco-GE-IR in June 1928. This large double-ended boxcab bore a strong resemblance to straight electric locomotives of the period. Fifty-two feet, one inch long, it weighed 150.5 tons and used a 2-D-2 wheel arrangement like New York Central's S-motor electrics designed 20 years earlier. Powering the locomotive was a 14.75x16-inch inline six-cylinder Ingersoll-Rand diesel engine that operated at 500 rpm and delivered 750 horsepower. Following a public exhibition in Atlantic City, it entered road-freight service tests on the Putnam division. A second experimental locomotive, No. 1500, was completed in July 1928. Intended for passenger service, this locomotive also used the 2-D-2 wheel arrangement but was even larger than the 1550—59 feet, 4 inches long—and weighed 180 tons. One of the significant accomplishments of this locomotive was its pioneering application of a McIntosh & Seymore diesel, a 14x18, 12-cylinder V-type engine that generated 900 horsepower at 310 rpm. McIntosh & Seymore engines became the standard for Alco diesel locomotives. This prototype also tested for a short while on the Putnam line, but was set aside in the mid-1930s.

Both locomotives performed well, fulfilling New York Central's expectations. But they were never duplicated. The onset of the Great Depression killed financing for the project, and by the time the economy had recovered, commercial diesels were being offered that matched the performance of these early experimentals. Furthermore, New York Central delayed dieselization as it refined its steam fleet in an effort to match diesel performance.

Westinghouse Diesels

Following the lead of Alco-GE-IR, Westinghouse entered the diesel-electric switcher market in 1926. Initially it produced a few boxcabs in conjunction with Brill, the Philadelphia-based streetcar and gas-electric railcar manufacturer. This arrangement was short-lived, and by the end of 1926 Westinghouse had ventured on its own into the diesel-electric field. Westinghouse relied on its electric locomotive partner, Baldwin, to supply mechanical gear. While Baldwin was also experimenting with diesels at this time, it had not yet developed them into a commercial venture. Westinghouse imported the Scottish Beardmore diesel engine and secured patent rights to build it in the United States. Westinghouse modified the Beardmore design as its locomotive business grew and it needed more powerful diesel engines. Arguably, the ultimate example of Westinghouse engine development was a 9x12-inch V-12, delivering 800 horsepower at 900 rpm.

Unlike Alco-GE-IR, which offered just two models, Westinghouse introduced a variety of different designs, including road freight and passenger locomotives. Its first customer was the Long Island, which ordered a pair of boxcabs in 1928. Later that year, Westinghouse built a pair of diesel-electric passenger locomotives for Canadian National's transcontinental passenger runs. They resembled straight electrics of the period, employing a 2-D-1+1-D-2 wheel arrangement.

In 1936, Westinghouse discontinued its diesel line when it entered a partnership with Baldwin, which formally entered the diesel market at this time. Westinghouse was in the diesel-electric business for less than 10 years, selling very few locomotives after the onset of the Depression, and its total production was just 29 diesel locomotives. Over that time, however, it made some important advances. In addition to its successful application of a diesel-electric road passenger locomotive, Westinghouse introduced what it called the "visibility cab"—a departure from the standard boxcab design. This inspired many later switcher designs employed by other manufacturers.

Electro-Motive: Railcars and Diesel Engines

Following World War I American railroads faced increasing highway competition. Branchlines and rural mainlines were particularly hard hit, and railroads were again looking for ways to dramatically reduce branchline operating

In 1931 General Electric and Ingersoll-Rand built seven 60-ton hood-style diesel-electric switchers for the Bush Terminal in Brooklyn, New York. They were powered by a six-cylinder 10x12-inch diesel that generated 300 horsepower. *C. J. Burger*

> ## WE'RE SELLING
> *a standard car engineered by us, and bearing a standard price tag."*
>
> —Electro-Motive, circa 1925 from *On Time* by Franklin M. Reck

Baltimore & Ohio's "Capitol Dome" emblem on pioneer EMC EA No. 51.

Baltimore & Ohio operated the first EMC E-units—the first streamlined diesel-electrics that were not permanently attached to an articulated train set. An EA/EB set leads No. 28 *The Columbian*, eastbound at Murikirk, Missouri, on August 6, 1939—less than a month before Germany invaded Poland, plunging the world into six years of war. *Bruce Fales, Jay Williams collection*

costs. This created a resurgence in the gas-electric railcar market that had dwindled during the war.

In 1922, Harold Hamilton, a man with a mix of railroad and automotive experience, helped found the Electro-Motive Engineering Corporation specifically to fill a need in the expanding railcar market. Hamilton hired a number of talented men, many of whom had once worked for General Electric's rail motorcar division, and gradually built up a brain trust. Although in 1923 the name of Hamilton's company was shortened to just Electro-Motive Company, its original title best described its true nature—an engineering firm. Electro-Motive primarily comprised engineers and salesmen, and unlike conventional railway equipment suppliers, Electro-Motive did not actually manufacture its product. Instead it designed and sold gas-electric railcars and coordinated subcontractors to build them, yet maintained tight control over the end product. It guaranteed the cars and supplied parts for them.

Electro-Motive relied on established passenger car builders, including the St. Louis Car Company and Pullman, to provide railcar bodies. General Electric was Electro-Motive's primary electrical supplier, and the companies enjoyed an especially close relationship because of their numerous personal connections. Electro-Motive's sole engine supplier was the Winton Engine Company, a producer of high-quality four-cycle gasoline engines.

Electro-Motive sold its first railcar in 1924, and by the end of the 1920s it dominated the railcar market. Many companies had tried their hand in the railway motorcar business, but most did not survive long. Even industrial giant General Electric exited the business after just a few years. What allowed Electro-Motive to excel was its unorthodox business strategy, strong sales technique, expert engineering, and a few technological developments that gave its products a distinct advantage over other designs. The use of gas-electric railcars offered a potentially dramatic cost advantage over conventional steam-powered branch-line trains. Poor reliability of many early cars, combined with the traditional pro-steam mind-set of many railroad managers, led to negative sentiments toward any internal-combustion-powered vehicle. To overcome this sales barrier, Hamilton bypassed conventional sales routines aimed at railroad motive power officials, and dealt directly with top decision makers. He offered them a way to save money at a time when they desperately needed to cut costs.

Electro-Motive broke with another industry convention: instead of custom designing its products to meet a specific railroad's requirements, Electro-Motive engineers designed and refined a standard product line for sale. This practice cut design costs, significantly reduced the price of individual railcars, and resulted in a better product. Customer suggestions, preferences, and design requirements were tested and then implemented on new models, but not on specific orders. Electro-Motive maintained very high quality standards and demanded the highest production quality from its suppliers.

Winton designed a series of new and progressively more powerful engines to power Electro-Motive railcars. In early 1925 Winton introduced a 225-horsepower gasoline engine,

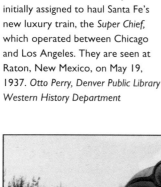

In 1935 EMC built two boxcab road diesels for Santa Fe. Popularly known as "The Twins," they were initially assigned to haul Santa Fe's new luxury train, the *Super Chief,* which operated between Chicago and Los Angeles. They are seen at Raton, New Mexico, on May 19, 1937. *Otto Perry, Denver Public Library Western History Department*

followed by a 275-horsepower engine later that year. By 1927, 300- and 400-horsepower engines were available. Electro-Motive was also able to take advantage of an improved control system designed by GE's Hermann Lemp. Instead of using several different levers to control engine speed and traction motor output, Lemp's system simplified and coordinated the control of the engine with traction motor output using a single throttle lever, allowing for maximum efficiency and ease of operation.

Electro-Motive quickly gained a reputation for producing very high quality railcars at a reasonable price, and by 1930 had captured more than 80 percent of the domestic railcar market. It sold more than 500 cars.

General Motors

In 1930, General Motors was looking to develop a commercially viable diesel engine. Rather than start from scratch, GM officials decided to purchase an existing engine company and build on its designs. GM acquired Winton, one of the most respected engine producers of the period. A short while later, GM also purchased Winton's primary customer, Electro-Motive, which was renamed the Electro-Motive Corporation and operated as an independently managed subsidiary within the GM corporate structure. GM was not necessarily interested in entering the railway business at that time, and it's not entirely clear why GM acquired the railcar manufacturer, but Electro-Motive's good reputation, its executives' shrewd marketing abilities, its high quality standards, and near domination of the railcar industry certainly contributed to GM's interest. Ironically, Electro-Motive's business vanished shortly after entering the GM fold. While Electro-Motive enjoyed great prosperity in the 1920s, as did most railway suppliers, including the three large steam locomotive manufacturers—Alco, Baldwin, and Lima—the onset of the Great Depression in 1929 precluded further investment in equipment. By 1932, the company had sold its last conventional railcar and its prospects looked dim.

In the early 1930s, the U.S. Navy was investigating diesel propulsion for submarines and was funding diesel research and development. General Motors was among several engine producers, including Fairbanks-Morse and Cooper-Bessemer, interested in benefiting from the Navy's business, and undertook substantial research and development despite the depressed civilian market. GM's Charles Kettering was in charge of research and worked with Winton to develop a lightweight, high-horsepower diesel.

Winton was no stranger to the diesel—it had built stationary diesel engines since 1913. Suffering from the same designs as most early diesels, however, Winton diesels were enormous, heavy machines with low output. Winton's W-40 weighed 45 tons (as much as some later diesel-electric switchers) and produced just 450 horsepower. It had a 200-pound-per-horsepower ratio, which

was much too low for either submarine or railway applications. The diesel engines' high compression ratio (typically 16 to 1) required to ignite the fuel needed extremely strong metals to contain the explosion within the cylinders. Traditionally, this required a large cast-iron or cast-steel block. To overcome the weight-strength problem, GM and Winton engineers took advantage of recently developed alloyed metals that were much lighter and stronger than conventional materials, and used modern welding techniques instead of casting. They combined this new technology with two other important innovations over earlier Winton engines: re-engineered fuel injectors and a practical, two-cycle diesel design.

The new system of fuel injection forced atomized fuel under pressure directly into the cylinder, eliminating the high-pressure fuel lines and external fuel delivery apparatus that had plagued earlier engine designs. But GM's major innovation was the complex engineering that produced a successful two-cycle engine.

Two-cycle Engines

Two-cycle internal combustion engines had been around for decades, but most practical engines used a four-cycle design. Winton traditionally employed a conventional four-cycle design. Seeking to develop greater power without a substantial weight increase, however, moved Kettering and his GM design group toward refining a two-cycle design.

Each piston motion, up or down, is described as a cycle or piston stroke. A four-cycle engine (or "four-stroke" engine) requires two complete crankshaft rotations and two up-and-down piston sequences of the pistons within the cylinders to complete a full combustion sequence. The first piston upstroke compresses air in the cylinder, raising its temperature to the combustion point. At the appropriate moment, diesel fuel is mechanically injected into the cylinder and under pressure ignites (the diesel does not require spark plugs for ignition, although some compression engines may use spark plugs for starting). The explosion thrusts the piston down, in the second cycle called a power stroke. In the third cycle (second upstroke) the piston forces exhausted gases from the cylinder, and during the fourth cycle draws fresh air into the cylinder, completing the sequence. A two-cycle engine accomplishes the full combustion sequence in just one crankshaft rotation. Forced air intake occurs during the first-half of the compression stroke; exhaust scavenging occurs during the second-half of the power stroke

A two-cycle engine obtains greater power than a four-cycle engine from a block of equal size—or, as GM applied the design, achieves the same power from a smaller engine. But the two-cycle design is less efficient, and results in significantly greater stress on engine components and increased wear. At the time of the Winton 201 development, diesel fuel was so inexpensive that poor fuel efficiency was not a significant factor. By contrast, today a half-percentage advantage in fuel economy can make the difference in locomotive sales.

Winton 201

The model 201 two-cycle diesel engine was the product of several years' research and development by GM and its Winton subsidiary. This engine embodied most of the characteristics that Kettering and his engineers had hoped to achieve. It was an eight-cylinder inline block, with 8x10-inch cylinders that operated at 750 rpm. Each cylinder produced 75 horsepower, for a total output of 600 horsepower. The engine produced about 20 horsepower per pound, making it roughly 10 times lighter than previous diesel engine designs—an order of magnitude improvement. It was ideally suited for railway use in addition to other intended applications. The first two 201 diesel engines were publicly displayed at the Century of Progress Exposition at Chicago in 1933.

Enter the Streamliners

By 1933, rail ridership had reached an all-time low for the century. Solid, heavyweight passenger cars hauled by conventional steam locomotives provided a reasonably comfortable, reliable mode of transportation, but had fallen out of fashion. Automobiles (and airplanes) had undeniable travel appeal—they were new, exciting, different, and often faster door-to-door. By the 1920s, automobiles had cut into railroad passenger revenues, but the Great Depression was devastating. For years travelers had been gradually abandoning the railroad in favor of other modes, but now they were avoiding trains completely. Something had to be done, and what could be a better business strategy than making trains new and exciting again? The idea was to make them more like cars and airplanes—sleek, fast, modern, and most of all, fashionable.

Until the early 1930s, the diesel locomotive was an obscure development that largely eluded the public eye. Railroad officials and readers of railway trade magazines had closely followed diesel developments, but the public was

Union Pacific's Streamliner, M10000, on its world-famous exhibition trip, March 3, 1934.
Otto Perry, Denver Public Library Western History Department

neither interested in nor aware of the application of diesel-electric locomotives on American rails. But then, rather suddenly, the diesel-electric took on a flashy new look and stepped out of the yard onto the mainline and into the popular media. So while in 1930 hardly anyone knew what a diesel-locomotive was, by 1935 almost everyone did!

While it might seem that the streamliner appeared out of nowhere in 1934, it really was an evolutionary coalescence of electric traction, gas-electric rail car, modern aircraft and automotive frame technologies applied to passenger car construction, and lightweight submarine diesels. A few progressive railcar designs also set the stage for something new and exciting.

In 1932 and 1933, Pullman, the long-time producer of railroad passenger cars, tried to resuscitate its floundering railcar business by constructing a highly unorthodox demonstrator designed by William B. Stout—an aeronautical designer better known for his popular Ford Tri-Motor airplane. The body of the car used a tubular welded frame covered by an aluminum skin. At that time aluminum was not readily associated with railroad construction, and the car was a featherweight, even by lightweight railcar standards. Measuring 60 feet long and weighing just 12.5 tons, about a third the weight of a conventional railcar the same size, it featured a sleek streamlined appearance, and looked like a cross between a wingless airplane and bloated McKeen car. Named *Railplane*, it was powered by two Waukesha six-cylinder gasoline engines and intended for 90-miles-per-hour operation.

At the same time as Pullman's *Railplane*, a similar initiative was undertaken by two apparent strangers to the American railroad market. An obscure Philadelphia-based auto-frame supplier called the Edward G. Budd Manufacturing Company and the French Michelin Rubber Company teamed up to construct a new kind of railcar that would ride on flanged, rubber tire–equipped wheels. Michelin had been marketing similar railcars in Europe since the 1920s and hoped to expand into the American market. Edward Budd had interest in the project because it appeared to be a logical extension of his business, and he had designed framing for McKeen cars in his early days. Budd and Michelin had initially built two demonstrators that incorporated a significant Budd-inspired innovation: shot-welded stainless-steel construction, developed to overcome frame failures on early McKeen cars. The resulting semi-streamlined, fluted stainless-steel design later became a hallmark of Budd-built products.

In 1933, Budd and Michelin constructed a two-section streamlined railcar for Texas & Pacific, sometimes cited as the first true streamlined passenger train. It embodied elements of the prototypes, although it was substantially heavier. The powercar used conventional steel wheels, while the trailer used Michelin's rubber tire innovation. Named the *Silver Slipper*, it was powered by a 240-horsepower gasoline engine. Despite its fresh appearance, it remained relatively obscure and never received the national media attention enjoyed by later streamlined trains. The heyday of the streamliner, however, was just around the corner. The Century of Progress Exposition in Chicago was the dynamic synergy that brought together all the right people to make the modern streamliner a reality. Among noteworthy exhibits included Pullman's *Railplane* and Winton's 201 diesel engine. Representatives of General Motors, Pullman, and Budd met with key railroad officials. Soon both Pullman and Budd were simultaneously tackling competing streamliner projects. Pullman worked with Union Pacific, and Budd with UP's arch rival, the Chicago, Burlington & Quincy (Burlington), while General Motors supplied the engines for both efforts.

Union Pacific's Streamliner

Consistent with national trends, Union Pacific had suffered dramatic passenger losses during the 1920s. Maury Klein reports in his book *Union Pacific (Vol. II)* that in 1929 passenger traffic reflected 60 percent of 1920 levels. By 1932, this figure had dropped to 23.6 percent of the peak. Federal regulations prevented the railroad from completely abandoning passenger service, and such a draconian move would not have been acceptable politically in the those hard times. The American public had a strong railroad awareness in the 1930s, and it would have been inconceivable for a major carrier such as Union Pacific to discontinue all passenger service, regardless of poor ridership statistics. So the railroad embarked on a plan that would significantly reduce costs while hopefully simultaneously attracting riders back to the rails.

The railroad wanted a train that could dramatically outperform existing steam-powered trains: it needed to run for

Union Pacific's *Streamliner* was a public sensation, attracting large crowds everywhere it went. Otto Perry photographed it in Denver surrounded by a curious and admiring public. This first streamliner was powered by a Winton distillate engine; later trains used diesels. *Otto Perry, Denver Public Library Western History Department*

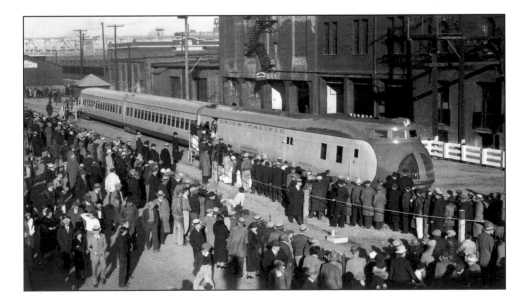

A Union Pacific promotional brochure from 1934 depicts the *Streamliner,* a futuristic-looking aluminum train, powered by a Winton engine. Union Pacific officials believed that the new streamliner would attract passengers back to the rails. They were right! *Richard Jay Solomon collection*

500 miles between fuel stops, maintain extremely high speeds, and shorten existing transcontinental runs by at least a day. It also wanted to accomplish this using less fuel, without a tremendous outlay of capital. The internal-combustion–powered streamliner fit this strategy, and Union Pacific pioneered the concept with help from Electro-Motive and Pullman. A decade earlier such desires would have been impossible to meet, but the recent advances in internal combustion technology and train design made UP's dream feasible.

Union Pacific had closely monitored developments in internal combustion technology over the years, and it was no stranger to the capabilities of the internal combustion engine. The pioneering gas-mechanical McKeen cars (see page 29) had been sponsored and promoted by Union Pacific's Edward H. Harriman. A. H. Fetters, a Union Pacific engineer who had worked with McKeen, had continued research into petroleum fuels in an effort to develop a better engine, and in 1926 Union Pacific sent him to Europe to learn about diesel developments. His work greatly influenced Union Pacific's pioneering development of the Streamliner trains. Using wind tunnel tests performed by the University of Michigan for the UP, Pullman expanded on the concept of its commercially unsuccessful Railplane, and produced an aluminum train of unprecedented proportions.

While Electro-Motive's two-cycle 201 diesel engine had been successfully demonstrated at the Century of Progress, it was not to power UP's *Streamliner*; Electro-Motive's distillate

engine was used instead. In his book *Dawn of the Diesel Age*, John Kirkland explains that Union Pacific and Burlington were racing to build the very first streamlined train. While Pullman's train was ready for service first, Winton's 201A two-cycle diesel was not, so rather than wait, Fetters elected to run UP's streamliner with the distillate engine, thereby beating Burlington to operating the first streamlined train in the United States. By the time Burlington's Budd-built *Zephyr* was finished, the first 201A diesel engine was ready to go. So while UP's Streamliner was unveiled first, Burlington did take the title of the first diesel-electric streamliner—a more important innovation. Nevertheless, both trains were developed simultaneously and made their debuts within a couple of months of each other.

The Streamliner's Public Debut

On February 12, 1934, Pullman delivered the first internal-combustion–powered, high-speed, streamlined, articulated passenger train to Union Pacific. Its futuristic, aerodynamic design delivered a revolutionary impact. The three-car *Streamliner* No. M10000 employed a lightweight tubular carbody—whereby the superstructure was supported by the underbody—covered by a thin, riveted aluminum skin. The three cars weighed a total of only 85 tons, roughly that of a single heavyweight passenger car. The cars were just 11 feet tall, two feet shorter than typical passenger equipment, and featured a remarkable low-slung profile, riding just 9.5 inches above the rail. Eight axles carried the entire consist: the train's three cars rode on just four trucks, rather than the six of a conventional train. Where the cars joined they rode on a bogey, which resulted in an articulated, semi-permanently coupled combination. This minimized slack action, reduced train oscillation, and significantly reduced the train's weight, eliminating several sets of wheels, couplers, and related equipment.

The cab of the train was at the front, perched above an immense mouthlike grille that resembled an ominous, alien face. There was no mistaking this train at the time of its inauguration: it bore no resemblance to conventional steam trains, or to its railcar heritage.

A 12-cylinder 600-horsepower Winton distillate engine, using spark ignition, powered the train. It could carry enough fuel to run 500 to 900 miles, and the train was tested at speeds up to 110 miles per hour. Furthermore, its fuel costs were less than one-third that of a comparable steam-powered train, a figure that greatly impressed Union Pacific officials.

At the *Streamliner*'s public debut, Union Pacific's Chairman, Averill Harriman, announced that the company would acquire two similar streamliners for transcontinental service. The *Streamliner* M10000 embarked on a 12,625-mile barnstorming publicity tour of the United States, traveling from city to city, awing the public and advertising the Union Pacific. People adored the new train, and UP was amazed at the vast trackside crowds that came to watch its sleek new Streamliner pass by. This was for more than just another train—it represented a vision of the future, and in the dark days of the Great Depression, it offered hope. An estimated two million people came to see the M10000, and innumerable dignitaries and public officials inspected the train, including Franklin D. Roosevelt, the newly elected President of the United States.

After the M10000 concluded its tour, it entered regular service on a 197-mile run between Kansas City, Missouri, and Salina, Kansas, as Union Pacific's *City of Salina*. M10000 was assigned to this comparatively obscure run because of its short, inflexible consist, which was not well suited for a heavily traveled route. Also UP wanted a test in low-profile service in the event of service difficulties in its early months. Compared to later trains, the M10000 had a remarkably short service life. It was doomed by its restricted capacity, problems with its Winton distillate engine, and the cost of replacing it with a diesel. Union Pacific retired the pioneer streamlined train on the eve of American involvement in World War II, in December 1941. The train had rolled roughly 900,000 miles in less than eight years. It was scrapped at Omaha, Nebraska, in 1942 with the wartime demand for aluminum at an all-time high.

Later in 1934, Union Pacific's six-car M10001 made its debut on the heels of its popular predecessor. The new train featured a 900-horsepower Winton 201A diesel engine, making it Union Pacific's first diesel-electric streamliner. It could not claim the title of the first diesel-electric streamliner—Burlington's *Zephyr* (discussed next) had that honor. But the train was proudly introduced as part of Union Pacific's passenger fleet. Unlike the M10000, which was strictly a coach train intended for short-distance service and demonstration runs, the M10001 was truly a long-distance train. It included three sleeping cars, making it the first diesel-powered streamlined sleeper train. On October 22, 1934, the M10001 departed Los Angeles and ran directly to New York City, taking just 56 hours and 55 minutes to make the transcontinental run. It arrived at New York Central's Grand Central Terminal on October 25 amidst great celebration. Today we can fly from New York to Los Angeles in just six hours, so a 56-hour journey doesn't seem terribly impressive, but it was an amazing feat in 1934. The train had beaten the previous speed record by roughly 14.4 hours, set in 1906 by E. H. Harriman on a special run, and was nearly a full day faster than regularly scheduled passenger trains of the time. Following the spectacular success of its streamliner prototypes, Union Pacific ordered several other articulated train sets with longer consists to handle significantly greater capacity.

Burlington's Zephyr

Burlington's *Zephyr* (later known as the Pioneer *Zephyr*) was a product of Burlington's and Budd's engineering teams and

In the 1930s "Progress" was the word of the day. A Union Pacific brochure portrays the new diesel-powered M10001, which operated as *The City of Portland*. UP's third streamlined train, number M10002, looked very similar and entered service as the *City of Los Angeles* on May 15, 1936. *Richard Jay Solomon collection*

a direct descendant of Budd's earlier railcar efforts, including his work with McKeen and various European endeavors. The design of the train was similar to that of UP's *Streamliner*. Like Union Pacific, Burlington desired an aerodynamic train shape that would facilitate high-speed operations. The railroad worked with the Massachusetts Institute of Technology performing comprehensive wind tunnel tests to produce the most efficient profile. Following the example of the *Silver Slipper*, Budd used a shot-welded stainless-steel frame and fluted stainless-steel sides for the *Zephyr's* construction. It employed a three-car articulated design for the same reasons as UP's *Streamliner*. It was 197 feet long and weighed 100 tons, slightly heavier than the aluminum *Streamliner*, but still significantly lighter than a typical three-car passenger train and steam locomotive. The *Zephyr* featured an unmistakable slanted "shovel nose" that contrasted sharply with Union Pacific's "mouthlike grille." (According to William D. Middleton, the shovel-nose design was derived from work on the Philadelphia & Western's high speed "Bullet Cars," third-rail electrics that operated between 69th Street in Philadelphia and Norristown.) The engineer rode up front, and was afforded an unobstructed view of the tracks through a row of forward-facing windows, an enormous improvement in visibility over conventional steam locomotives (but a potential safety hazard for the crew, as the thin sheet metal offered little protection in the event of a collision).

Budd unveiled the pioneering *Zephyr* streamliner in Philadelphia, Pennsylvania, on April 18, 1934, less than two

The last Union Pacific articulated streamliners were M10004, M10005, and M10006 for service on the *City of Denver*. These trains featured a different cab styling and were much longer than the original *Streamliner*—operating with 12 to 14 cars, as opposed to just three. East of Denver, on February 16, 1937, M10005 passes an approach signal at an estimated 40 miles per hour. *Otto Perry, Denver Public Library Western History Department*

The *Twin Cities Zephyr* at St. Paul Union Station. The Budd-built *Pioneer Zephyr* spurred a whole family of similar trains using shovel-nose streamlined EMC powercars. *Tim Doherty collection*

months after UP's debut. Before the *Zephyr* went west to Chicago to roll on home rails, it toured in the East, showing off to the curious crowds. The *Zephyr*, numbered CB&Q 9900, received Winton's first production eight-cylinder 201A diesel engine, making it the very first diesel-electric streamliner. The spectacular success of the *Zephyr* with its Winton diesel was a great achievement for General Motors' engineering forces, and set an important precedent for further diesel applications.

Like the *Streamliner*, the speeding *Zephyr* was an unusual spectacle, and people were eager to catch a glimpse of it as the train whisked by. Aesthetically speaking, the *Zephyr* was a far more striking train. Its shining stainless-steel body glistened in the sun, and shone on its own even on dull days. The *Zephyr* looked like it moved fast, and its tail-end observation lounge—a feature not found on its competition—provided an extraordinary view of the tracks and passing scenery. The *Zephyr's* timeless streamlined treatment still looks modern today, more than 65 years after its debut, and resembles modern streamlined trains in Europe and Japan.

In the spring of 1934, Burlington's *Zephyr* was big news and, like M10000, spawned a fleet of similar trains with more powerful powercars and longer consists. After the fair, the *Zephyr* entered regular service, often running as the *Denver Zephyr* between Chicago and the "Mile High City."

More Streamliners

The success of the *Streamliner* and the *Zephyr* led many other railroads around the United States to introduce streamlined trains of their own. While some chose to follow the example of Union Pacific and Burlington by embracing internal combustion technology, others chose to remain with more conventional power. At the same time UP and CB&Q were displaying their wondrous new trains, Pennsylvania Railroad was testing its latest electric locomotive designs, the R1 and GG1 electrics, which also used a streamlined design. Also in 1934, New York Central

followed the advice of a young graduate student named Norman Zapf and applied wind-resistant streamlined shrouds to one of its powerful J-1a Hudson-type steam locomotives in an effort to improve performance. In a similar vein, in 1935 Milwaukee Road ordered a very small fleet of aerodynamic-inspired streamlined Atlantic types for its high-speed *Hiawatha* trains between Chicago, Milwaukee, and the Twin Cities. These were the first new American-built streamlined steam locomotives. Numerous other lines applied streamlined shrouds to their steam locomotives, or ordered new streamlined steam engines as a way of sprucing up their image.

While some lines were dressing up steam engines, and others ordering custom-designed diesel-electric streamliners, Boston & Maine was quite happy with Burlington's

The *Denver Zephyr* hits 80 miles per hour at Barr, Colorado, on March 6, 1937. Burlington operated a whole fleet of EMC-powered Budd-built *Zephyrs* based on the successful design of the *Pioneer Zephyr*. Later trains were longer and more flexible than the original. *Otto Perry, Denver Public Library Western History Department*

Boston & Maine bought a near duplicate of Burlington's *Pioneer Zephyr.* It carried the number 6000, and was initially assigned to the *Flying Yankee,* which ran from Boston's North Station to Portland and Bangor, Maine, over B&M and Maine Central. While it later worked a variety of other assignments, including *The Mountaineer* to New Hampshire's White Mountains, it is seen here at North Station on July 6, 1940. *Carleton Parker, courtesy of Bob's Photo*

No. Sta. B+M Boston July 6-1940
The Mountaineer lv. for White Mts.

New Haven's *Comet* operated between Boston and Providence, Rhode Island, on New Haven's mainline. Typically it made five trips daily. While New Haven considered purchasing a fleet of similar trains and other railroads also considered the design, it was never replicated. After roughly 15 years of service it was retired. *Carleton Parker, courtesy of Bob's Photo*

Comet at Canton Jct. July 21-1935

Zephyr design, so it ordered a virtual duplicate of the pioneering articulated train. On April Fool's Day 1935, less than a year after the unveiling of the *Zephyr*, B&M introduced its own EMC-powered, Budd-built, shovel-nosed, stainless-steel train, initially working as the *Flying Yankee*.

New Haven's *Comet*, a three-car, double-ended, articulated streamlined train set, was introduced in 1935. This unique train, known as the *Rail Zepplin*, employed a wind-tunnel design and was built by Goodyear using an aluminum body. Powered by a Westinghouse diesel engine, the whole train weighed just 126 tons, about 40 percent of a comparable steam train of the period, and was capable of operating at speeds up to 109 miles per hour.

Gulf Mobile & Northern's first streamlined *Rebel* trains entered service in July 1935 between Jackson, Tennessee, and New Orleans. Unlike the other streamliners, these trains were not articulated, and regularly swapped a center car to adjust for ridership differences. Styled by renowned industrial designer Otto Kuhler, the *Rebel* trains were built by American Car & Foundry at Berwick, Pennsylvania, and used Alco's 600-horsepower McIntosh & Seymore 531 engine and Westinghouse electrical gear. The last *Rebel* train entered service in September 1937.

The last of the 1930s internal combustion-electric articulated streamliners was Illinois Central's fierce-looking *Green Diamond*. It was a five-car Pullman-built, EMC-powered streamliner that reflected automotive styling of the period and bore a family resemblance to UP's Pullman streamliners. The *Green Diamond* was inaugurated on May 17, 1936, and operated primarily on IC's Chicago-St. Louis route.

Articulation, No; Diesels, Yes!

Though articulation allowed for weight reduction, provided a smoother ride at high speed, and aided in very high speed running, the concept was quickly frowned upon by railroad operating men. The early articulated train sets suffered from inflexibility. Fixed train sets did not allow railroads to adjust the consist as patronage ebbed and flowed. This proved especially difficult when the new streamlined trains suffered from their own success, attracting much larger passenger counts than they could handle. The railroads were forced to accommodate overflow patrons on regular steam-powered trains—defeating the streamlined concept as far as the riding public was concerned. Also, while diesels had a better reliability record than steam, if there was a serious problem with a streamliner's powercar (or any other part of the train for that matter), the entire consist needed to be removed from service while repairs were made. The railroad was unable to simply provide a substitute locomotive, as it would with a conventional train.

But the diesel had made its mark, and only a short time after the streamliner prototypes had toured the United States, EMC began marketing passenger diesel-electrics as

separate locomotives with conventional couplers, capable of hauling any passenger consist, not just specialized streamlined trains. Meanwhile, the articulated train concept quietly slipped into the shadows. By 1937, no one was ordering articulated streamliners any more, although the gimmick tended to re-emerge from time to time as a way of attracting the support of new riders, politicians, and the media.

Issued April 26, 1959

FLORIDA EAST COAST *Railway*

TIME TABLES

FLORIDA'S ONLY DOUBLE TRACK ROUTE

While streamlined trains caught on, articulation was quickly dropped. A 1959 Florida East Coast passenger timetable portrays a set of Electro-Motive E7 diesels on a passenger train. Streamlined diesels based on the aesthetic considerations of the early streamliners were built through the 1950s. *Richard Jay Solomon collection*

3

ELECTRO-MOTIVE BUILDS DIESELS

DESPITE THE SPECTACULAR SUCCESS of the lightweight streamliners, GM initially exhibited some reservations about entering the diesel locomotive business. The railroads were still suffering from traffic doldrums because of the Depression, and few were making significant locomotive purchases. Yet the streamliners had a threefold impact on the future of GM diesel production. They convinced the railroads, the public, and GM that diesels were the future of American railroads. General Motors overcame its reservations as engineers at Electro-Motive convinced top management of the great potential market for EMC products if provided with proper backing for research, development, marketing, and construction facilities. General Motors was the world's largest industrial company, and in 1935, a year after the introduction of the streamliners and more than four years after it purchased Electro-Motive, GM made a firm financial commitment to large-scale diesel locomotive production.

GM's substantial financial backing provided EMC with sufficient resources to develop practical road diesel technology. And it changed the way American railroads operated trains. The potential for diesel locomotive sales was enormous: in the mid-1930s, the estimated cost of complete conversion of American railroads to diesel operation was $4 billion. Nevertheless, GM's investment represented a substantial undertaking for a Depression-era industry based on an undeveloped product line. Electro-Motive had relied on subcontractors for the construction of its products for more than a decade. It finally built its own locomotive shops, located at La Grange, Illinois, a few miles west of Chicago. While its new facility was being built, Electro-Motive built diesel-electric locomotives using its traditional production methods and contracted work to existing suppliers. It needed a diesel-electric demonstrator to use as a sales example to show railroads the capability of Electro-Motive products. The streamliners may have convinced a few lines that the diesel engine could whisk lightweight trains at high speed, but many in the industry remained skeptical. Yet two railroads, the Baltimore & Ohio, and longtime Electro-Motive railcar customer Santa Fe, were so eager to try diesel power that they asked EMC to build them road locomotives before the demonstrators were ready. So EMC built five boxcab road diesels—two demonstrators, and three for its customers. All five featured carbodies with B-B wheel arrangement, powered with dual Winton 201A V-12 diesels generating a combined output of 1,800 horsepower per locomotive.

The Erie Mining was built between 1954 and 1957 to transport iron ore from mines in the Minnesota Iron Range to Taconite Harbor, Minnesota, located on the northwest shore of Lake Superior. By the late 1990s this line, now operated by LTV Mining, was the last place in North America where F-units regularly hauled freight in traditional A-B-B-A sets.

EMC's boxcab demonstrators, designated Nos. 511 and 512, were assembled at GE's Erie plant. Each unit weighed 240,000 pounds; the units were typically used as a 3,600-horsepower pair, a sufficiently powerful combination to haul conventional long-distance passenger trains. In *On Time*, author Franklin Reck indicates that the boxcab demonstrators burned 2.7 gallons of diesel per mile when hauling a typical 12- to 14-car passenger train, and based on contemporary coal and oil prices, the boxcabs produced a 40 to 60 percent fuel savings over steam. These unimpressive-looking locomotives were Electro-Motive's debut as a locomotive producer. It wasn't just building power cars anymore.

Although Santa Fe did not order any of the early streamliners, it was intrigued by the prospect of dieselization and envisioned diesel-electric power as a way to cut costs on its desert operations, where water procurement for steam locomotives was difficult and expensive. Santa Fe's EMC boxcabs, known popularly as The Twins, were similar to the 511-512 demonstrators, except they received some nominal styling. They are generally considered the first commercially built high-speed passenger diesels. In May 1936 Santa Fe assigned its EMC boxcabs to its newest luxury train, a weekly all-heavyweight Pullman-sleeper, called the *Super Chief*, run from Chicago to Los Angeles. With diesel power the train was able to make the 2,000-mile trek in just 39 hours and 45 minutes—15 hours faster than the best steam-powered run.

While not as flashy as the streamliners, the boxcabs demonstrated the advantages of diesel-electric locomotives and did not suffer by being permanently coupled to a fixed train set, giving them all the flexibility of a conventional locomotive. They could be operated together as a single 3,600-horsepower locomotive, or separated and used individually. Baltimore & Ohio used its single 1,800-horsepower boxcab on its fancy *Royal Blue*, the premier New York to Washington train.

Electro-Motive Designations

Electro-Motive locomotive designations are not as descriptive as those of other builders, and sometimes confusion and controversy arise as a result of inconsistencies in the meaning of prefix and suffix designations. Electro-Motive uses a letter and number combination, sometimes followed

Electro-Motive size comparison on the former Western Pacific: rolling westward through the Feather River Canyon at the Honeymoon Tunnels, Union Pacific's DDA40X 6936 leads the preserved FT A-B set on its way to Railfair '91 in Sacramento, California.

Early Electro-Motive Prefix Designations

Prefix	Indication
BL	Branchline
E	cab unit with A-1-A trucks, originally \ indicated 1,800 horsepower
F	cab unit with B-B trucks
FT	cab unit, Freight
FP	cab unit for Passenger service (equipped with a steam generator)
NC	Nine hundred horsepower, cast frame
NW	Nine hundred horsepower, welded frame
SC	Six hundred horsepower, cast frame
SW	Six hundred horsepower, welded frame (unofficially implied a switcher)
T	Transfer locomotive

Later Electro-Motive Prefix Designations

Prefix	Meaning
DD	Eight-axle locomotive with 'D' trucks
F	cowl locomotive (protective carbody)
GP	General Purpose (road switcher with B-B wheel arrangement)
SD	Special Duty (road switcher with C-C wheel arrangement)
P	Passenger
SW	Switcher

Suffix	Meaning
A	cab unit (locomotive with controls)
AC	Alternating current electrical systems
B	booster unit (locomotive without engineer controls)
C	for six-axle trucks (such as the F40C)
F	cowl/cab locomotive (a protective carbody)
I	Isolated cab
M	Safety cab
PH	passenger locomotive with headend power
T	Tunnel (air intakes located on the running boards)

by a letter suffix to indicate a model variation. There are often large gaps between Electro-Motive model numbers: for example, Electro-Motive produced GP7s, GP9s, and GP18s, but no GP12s or GP13s. Electro-Motive has variously inserted a hyphen between its letter prefix and number, but today Electro-Motive designations are generally written without hyphens, except for "dash 2" designations introduced in 1972, for example SD40-2.

Diesel Switchers

EMC had invested most of its early diesel efforts in high-speed passenger train powercars, but the largest established market for diesel locomotives was for yard switchers. Once it was ready to begin regular production at its new La Grange, Illinois, plant, the bulk of EMC's early business was in switchers. Initially, it built two basic types, a 600-horsepower locomotive, using an eight-cylinder Winton 201A, and a 900-horsepower locomotive powered by a 12-cylinder Winton 201A. Several different models were introduced reflecting various specification differences. The SC was a 600-horsepower locomotive that used a cast frame, while the SW, also 600 horsepower, used a welded frame. The NC and NW models followed a similar pattern.

The switcher market quickly proved very lucrative. During 1936, EMC built 56 locomotives, nearly as many as the combined totals of GE-IR and Westinghouse for the previous decade! The following year EMC built 94 diesels.

Enter the E-Unit

The boxcab demonstrators accomplished their mission and generated great interest in Electro-Motive diesels. They also served as a valuable test bed for EMC engineers to learn more about road diesels. At the time, this was unexplored

Freshly painted Rochester & Southern EMD-built SW1200 No. 107 basks in the sun at Brooks Avenue Yard in Rochester, New York, on the morning of September 23, 1987. The switcher's full lighting package, including both red and white oscillating headlights, reveals this locomotive's Southern Pacific heritage. Rochester & Southern is a Genesee & Wyoming family railroad created in 1986 to operate the former Baltimore & Ohio line to Rochester.

territory and in order to produce commercially viable road diesels, EMC needed to refine its product and work out flaws. Every new technology develops problems, and the successful application of a technological innovation requires practical solutions and patience before it will work reliably. Diesels were competing against well-established steam technology with more than 100 years of development behind it. While the 511 and 512 impressed some railway officials, they suffered from innumerable flaws that EMC needed to address. One of the most significant locomotive performance problems was the Winton 201 diesel engine itself. Electro-Motive decided to correct this by designing a whole new engine (see 567 Engine below), yet this took a couple of years and in the meantime the 201A was still the preferred prime mover.

Using their experience EMC engineers, under the direction of Dick Dilworth, went about designing an all-new passenger locomotive embodying the best qualities of its demonstrators and streamliners, while incorporating numerous suggestions from interested railroads. The new locomotive was intended to match performance characteristics of the best Hudson-type steam locomotive—considered by many the most advanced locomotive design of its time. Electro-Motive hoped to create a locomotive that would change the way most railroads moved passengers. In the mid-1930s, the streamliners caught the public's imagination, but only accounted for a small number of riders overall; most were still riding behind steam. Within a decade Electro-Motive changed that.

The new locomotive balanced a variety of considerations. The cab arrangement at the front of the locomotive used on the Burlington streamliners had proved problematic and needed to be changed. While many electrics and diesel-electrics had taken advantage of the front-end cab design—and this arrangement worked well for slow-speed switchers—operating at high speeds posed a different situation. Riding up front placed train crews in a perilous position in the event of collision. In the early 1930s, a Pennsylvania Railroad P5 electric boxcab had suffered a fatal crash that resulted in the redesigning of PRR's electrics to a center cab configuration, as used by the famous GG1, among other locomotives. A Burlington shovel-nose *Zephyr* suffered from a similar accident.

Electro-Motive responded by moving the operators' position away from the front, and changing the flat front surface used on the boxcabs to a reinforced rounded nose designed to deflect objects that struck the front of the train. The engineer rode at an elevated position that provided great forward visibility, while the nose shielded the view of tracks passing below, minimizing the chances that a crew would become mesmerized by the passing cross-ties, a psychological phenomenon termed "train nystagmus." Moving the cab required a strategic rearranging of crucial locomotive components including the engine and main generators. The cab and rounded nose modifications were concurrent with a new frame design and a change to the locomotive body structure.

The body was redesigned as an integral part of the support structure, instead of just an external shell supported by it.

To address crews' complaints about the large grilles used on EMC's Pullman streamliners—the aesthetically impressive air intake system had forced debris, insects, and even birds and small animals struck by the train into the engine compartment, making a mess that requiring constant cleaning—air intake vents were relocated to the sides of the locomotive. The new carbody made its debut in 1937 as the legendary E unit, employing a distinctive, pleasing styling that took its cue from the later streamliner powercars.

Early E's

The first E unit customers were those railroads most familiar with Electro-Motive diesels—Baltimore & Ohio, Santa Fe, and Union Pacific. The B&O received the very first commercially produced streamlined passenger diesel-electrics: 12 model EA/EBs. The EA ("A" units, cab units) featured a graceful sloping nose with inset headlight and a stylish blue and gray paint scheme. In May 1937, Santa Fe received the first of its 11 E1A/Bs delivered to haul its all new Budd-built streamlined passenger cars. The E1s employed a similar body style to the EAs, but were dressed in an unmistakable flashy red, yellow, black, and silver paint scheme now universally known as the "Santa Fe Warbonnet." This scheme, the work of Electro-Motive designer Leland A. Knickerbocker, was specifically intended for the stylish streamlined E1s. It was applied to numerous other locomotives over the years and remains among the most recognizable of railroad paint schemes.

Designing colorful paint schemes became an Electro-Motive specialty. In the steam era most locomotives were painted black and passenger cars were adorned in "Pullman Green"—a dark olive drab best suited for not looking dirty after a long trip. Diesels did not spew soot, so they could be painted a variety of bright colors. Many of EMD's schemes were adopted as formal color schemes by the railroads and applied to different diesels, often other than EMD's own.

Union Pacific took delivery of six distinctively styled E2A/Bs. Like the later streamliner power cars, they featured a bulbous front end and rows of porthole windows, but lacked the distinctive grille. All the early Es were powered by two 900-horsepower Winton 201A V-12 engines. EMC continued to implement design improvements, and the early Es were followed by hundreds of similar locomotives built to an improved standardized design that used a more reliable prime mover: EMC's 567 engine.

The 567 Engine

Although the Winton 201A engine's compact size and power output were vastly superior to earlier designs, it was intended, after all, for submarines, so by the mid-1930s Electro-Motive set out to design a diesel specifically for railroad locomotives.

Electro-Motive essentially invented the American passenger diesel. Its streamlined E-units were an outgrowth of the early articulated streamlined trains built in the early 1930s. After World War II the E-unit became the standard America passenger locomotive. In July 1958 near Chicago Union Station, a Baltimore & Ohio E8A and older E pause, as a pair of Pennsylvania Railroad E7As roll below. The E7s are identified by featuring both the "bulldog nose" and rectangular side windows (instead of round), while E8s and E9s both used round side windows, and earlier Es featured a steeply pitched nose. *Richard Jay Solomon*

Boston & Maine found that four FTs in an A-B-B-A set were too powerful for many trains, so it split the sets into A-B pairs. In 1948, a pair of FTs are captured approaching the west portal of the Hoosac Tunnel. *Robert A. Buck*

Winton diesel engines required an inordinate amount of running maintenance, and as the streamliners raced across the plains and prairies, impressing onlookers and passengers alike, there was a sideshow to the diesel drama unseen by the public. Electro-Motive engineers typically rode every run to ensure that the engines functioned properly. Piston heads and rods were routinely changed at terminals to compensate for high wear rates experienced as a result of constant high-speed running. It was not uncommon for engines to fail en route, and for EMC engineers to perform heavy repairs at speed, while the train rolled along on its remaining engines. Most of the early streamliners had at least four Winton engines, so delays were usually minimal. A failure was often an adventure for the engineers, who had to change out failed piston heads and broken rods, among other repairs, while rolling along at high speed. The enclosed carbody kept rain and wind from interfering with their labors.

Electro-Motive's 567 engine was an entirely new design that marked significant improvements in performance and reliability over the Winton 201A. The 567's piston bore was 8.5 inches, compared to 8 inches on the 201, and operating speed increased from 750 rpm to 800 rpm. (The designation 567 stems from 567 cubic inches of cylinder displacement. Electro-Motive has maintained this method of engine designation, and marks model modifications with a suffix.) Other 201 flaws, such as crankshaft, bearing, pushrod, and piston ring deficiencies, were also corrected. Components were designed to be interchangeable between different size engines, and the cylinder assemblies were easily removed and exchanged. At the end of 1938, the 567 engine supplanted the 201A on EMC's passenger line.

Better E's

Electro-Motive introduced its new 2,000 horsepower E-units in 1938. Four models, E3, E4, E5, and E6, incorporated a number of improvements over earlier models, including the new 567 engine. There was little difference between the E3, E4, and E6, while the E5 was distinguished by distinctive stainless-steel styling at the request of the Burlington—the sole purchaser of the model.

The F-Unit: Electro-Motive Moves Freight

Electro-Motive quickly dominated the new diesel business. It had the lion's share of the diesel switcher market, and basically invented the commercial passenger diesel. The next logical step was to tackle the heavy freight market, which represented the largest share of locomotive production. It was in this area that Electro-Motive stood to reap the largest profit, but this market was also the most difficult to sell to the railroads. In the eyes of many railroaders, switching freight cars and hauling comparatively lightweight passenger trains was one business, but moving freight tonnage was another. Hauling freight required real power—locomotives capable of moving a 4,000-ton train at sustained mainline speeds. In 1937, no diesel built by Electro-Motive or any other manufacturer could meet that demand. There was some skepticism but not all railroads were pessimistic, and according to Albert Churella in his book *From Steam to Diesel*, some lines encouraged Electro-Motive to enter the freight locomotive market.

Starting with its successful E-unit and the new 567 engine, Electro-Motive set out to design a freight locomotive that was suited to the task—a locomotive capable of hauling heavy freight trains in rugged territory. In November 1939, Electro-Motive unveiled a locomotive that met these challenges, changing the way railroaders viewed diesel-electrics, and in a short time changing the way America moved freight. This was the four-unit, 5,400-horsepower, streamlined model FT, the first of Electro-Motive's F-units.

The FT demonstrator was number 103, painted in dark green and mustard yellow. Its four units—two A-unit cabs, bracketing two B-unit boosters—each contained a prime mover, Electro-Motive's 16-cylinder 567 engine. The 567 generated 1,350 horsepower—more than double the output of the early Winton engines. The A-units were 48 feet, 3 inches long, while B-units measured just 48 feet, one inch. Each rode on a pair of newly designed Blomberg trucks, which incorporated a spring suspension system similar to that used on the A1A Blomberg trucks on EMC's E units. The Blomberg truck used a system of outside swing hangers and a mix of elliptical and helical springs, providing great stability at speed while enabling the locomotive to negotiate extremely tight curves. The cabs were the first locomotives to feature Electro-Motive's famous "bulldog nose," a more conservative streamlining treatment than the sloping front

In 1947 a pair of FTs rolls westward, approaching the east portal of the 4.75-mile long Hoosac Tunnel. The tunnel was once electrified, but Boston & Maine discontinued electric operations following the arrival of the E7s in 1946; freights were dieselized with FTs in 1943–1944. *Robert A. Buck*

In 1951 a Boston & Maine F2A leading an A-B FT set approaches the east portal of the Hoosac Tunnel. Three units were better suited for B&M's application, but the semi-permanently coupled A-B sets could not be separated, so B&M bought F2As to operate A-B-A sets. *Robert A. Buck*

used on the early E-units. Connecting the cabs and booster, EMC substituted drawbars in the place of knuckle couplers, intending the A-B sets to always operate together as pairs, interdependent on one another. For example, the batteries for both units were located in the B-unit, while the only control stand was located in the A-unit. Furthermore, by coupling the locomotives that way, Electro-Motive, along with its customers, hoped to avoid labor issues involving multiple-unit operation.

Electro-Motive now offered a diesel-electric in every major locomotive category, giving the company a unique position among American locomotive producers. Electro-Motive wasted little time in showing off its new product and the FT began its famous barnstorming tour around the United States. In the course of 11 months it covered nearly 84,000 miles, operating on 20 Class I carriers through 35 states. Among the railroads it visited were the Santa Fe, B&O, and CB&Q, which had been early EMC diesel customers. While the FT's performance cannot be described as flawless (the locomotive had its fair share of difficulties), it impressed most of the roads it tested on. Though at 5,400 horsepower its power output did not exceed many steam locomotives, the four-unit FT set was capable of delivering a greater starting tractive effort than many of the most powerful steam locomotives. Furthermore

The streamlined, articulated train gets reinvented every couple of decades. In the mid-1950s, 20 years after the *Zephyr* and *Streamliner* toured the country, a whole new generation of lightweight streamliners made their debut. General Motors' concept was the *Aerotrain*, essentially a powercar hauling bus bodies on steel wheels. Despite futuristic styling, the train failed. Three Aerotrain locomotives were built, and ultimately all ended up in Rock Island suburban service where one is seen here in June 1961. *Richard Jay Solomon*

the FT offered a feature that steam was not capable of: dynamic braking. Some electric locomotives had employed regenerative braking systems that embodied the same concept as dynamic braking, whereby traction motors could be converted to electric generators to slow the train down. With regenerative braking, the electricity generated was returned to the power grid through the catenary, but dynamic braking on diesel-electrics sent the current to electric resistor grids that converted it to heat, which was then dissipated into the air using blowers. While this was a less efficient use of energy, it was very useful in controlling long freight trains and reducing brakeshoe wear.

Santa Fe was especially impressed—not surprising, considering it had been one of the first to purchase Electro-Motive boxcabs, E-units, and switchers. Santa Fe saw the FT as nearly the perfect locomotive to allow it to eliminate steam operations from its troublesome desert lines, and it was the first railroad to place an order for FTs. However, Santa Fe was unhappy with the drawbar connection between the cab and booster, having recognized that this would result in locomotive assignment difficulties, and the

company insisted on conventional couplers instead. Electro-Motive complied with Santa Fe's request, although most FTs for other customers were delivered with drawbar connections, a feature that predictably resulted in numerous operational headaches in later years. Santa Fe's first FTs were built at the end of 1940 and entered revenue service in February 1941.

The FT permitted Santa Fe to banish steam from its 460-mile mainline segment across the Arizona and California desert between Winslow and Barstow, making this one of the first long portions of American mainline to boast of complete dieselization—a fact that undoubtedly pleased both Santa Fe and Electro-Motive officials. This line included one of the longest unbroken grades in the United States, the long climb from the Colorado River east of Needles, which marks the boundary between California and Arizona, to the summit at Flagstaff. In addition to solving its water and fueling problems, Santa Fe found that FTs were far more capable of handling freight than even its most modern steam locomotives. One source states that FTs could haul 3,500 tons on this run, compared to just 2,000 tons with Santa Fe's best

steam power. This was good for Electro-Motive and a warning sign for the steam manufacturers.

On January 1, 1941, as the FT was beginning production, General Motors reorganized the Electro-Motive Corporation as its Electro-Motive Division (EMD). Since then EMD has become synonymous with diesel-electric locomotives, producing tens of thousands of locomotives for service around the world.

The FT was a phenomenal business success. It was a practical alternative to steam. Furthermore, diesels could also be used as an alternative to electrification. Twenty-three American railroads ordered FTs, and although production was temporarily suspended in 1943 (because EMD facilities were needed to produce submarine engines for the war effort), a total of 555 A-units and 541 B-units were built between 1939 and 1945. Santa Fe owned the largest roster, with 320 locomotives, followed by the Great Northern with 96, and the Southern Railway with 76 (including those owned by Southern subsidiaries).

The FT was marketed as a four-unit, 5,400-horsepower freight locomotive, but many railroads ordered FTs with steam generators suitable for passenger service, and some lines used them in dual service. For a short time Santa Fe had 11 four-unit sets geared for 90-mile-per-hour operation and dressed in the passenger Warbonnet paint scheme. They were later regeared for freight service. Many lines separated the original A-B-B-A FT sets into A-B sets, and a few ordered A-B-A sets. The inflexibility of the drawbar connection proved to be unacceptable to many railroads and was not used on later F models.

More F-Units

With the conclusion of the war, EMD introduced an improved line of F-units, correcting difficulties encountered with the FTs, and aiming to satisfy a postwar market environment. The success of the FT, combined with EMD's excellent reputation, shrewd marketing skills, and mass-production capabilities, guaranteed the popularity of its F-unit line. North American railroads embraced the F, buying them by the thousands in the postwar years. In just a short time, the F-unit had become the new standard American locomotive employed in a great variety of mainline services. It could be found from the forests of northern Maine to the California coast. F-units were used to haul heavy ore drags in the

Minnesota Iron Range, race fast "Piggyback" intermodal trains across the Southwest, and bring luxurious streamlined passenger trains from the Pacific coast to the Midwest. The F was known by a variety of nicknames including "Cabs" and "Covered Wagons," and almost every Class I railroad in the United States used them in one capacity or another.

EMD demonstrated its 1,500-horsepower F3 in 1945, using an improved diesel engine designated 567B. EMD was unable to begin immediate production, so for a short time after the war it sold an interim 1,350-horsepower model designated F2. Some railroads, such as Boston & Maine, purchased small fleets of F2As to pair with separated A-B FTs, permitting A-B-A locomotive sets. The F2 was only produced for a few months in 1946 until the F3 was ready for mass production.

The F3 reflected a variety of improvements over the FT gained through World War II service experience when EMD was not permitted to make major design changes. The F3 used a new generator and replaced belt-driven and mechanically driven internal appliances with electrically powered units, increasing overall reliability while reducing maintenance costs.

EMD offered the F3 in eight different gear ratios, allowing railroads to select the most efficient power arrangement for their intended application. Using a 56:21 ratio permitted a maximum safe speed of 102 miles per hour but only 21,000 pounds maximum continuous tractive effort, an arrangement

well suited for high-speed passenger service, but not practical for most heavy freight applications. On the other end of the spectrum, a 65:12 gear ratio only allowed for a maximum speed of 50 miles per hour, but produced 42,500 pounds maximum continuous tractive effort, ideal for slow-speed drag service. Most F3s used a gear ratio between these two extremes. EMD produced the F3 until February 1949 (when it introduced the F7), building a total of 1,111 F3As and 696 F3Bs. This was a large portion of the total production at the company's La Grange, Illinois, plant at that time.

The F7 resembled the F3 in its outward appearance, but it embodied numerous design improvements that resulted in a more reliable, productive locomotive. EMD's new D-27 traction motor design allowed the F7 to generate slightly greater tractive effort at low speeds by extending short time ratings (thus permitting the locomotive to operate a maximum load longer without damaging traction motors). A fuel injector redesign permitted the use of a cheaper, lower grade of diesel fuel, and improved dynamic brakes made for easier train handling. EMD also introduced the FP7, which featured a carbody four feet longer than the F7 in order to accommodate a steam generator and larger boiler for passenger service.

In the early 1950s, EMD's competition boosted the output of most road locomotives from 1,500 horsepower to 1,600 horsepower. EMD did not immediately react to this trend, yet its locomotives still dominated the market, outselling everything else offered by the other builders. A power race was on, and Baldwin, Fairbanks-Morse, and Alco gradually pushed up the threshold, offering increasingly more powerful freight locomotives. By 1953, Fairbanks-Morse and Alco were both offering road-switchers that produced between 2,250 horsepower and 2,400 horsepower, significantly more than EMD's most powerful locomotives. Yet, despite this great power advantage, these high-horsepower locomotives did not enjoy brisk sales. In 1954, EMD introduced several new locomotive models, including its F9 and FP9, which used the new 567C engine working at 835 rpm (compared to earlier engines that worked at 800 rpm) and produced 1,750 horsepower, an increase of 250 horsepower over earlier models.

The F9 was the last regular F-unit model offered. The passenger version FP9 was not popular in the United States but did capture a small market in Canada and Mexico. In 1956, EMD designed a specialized dual-mode diesel-electric/electric, the FL9, for the New Haven (see sidebar).

The F-unit reign was intense but short. EMD built roughly 7,600 F-units in a 20-year span. In the early 1950s, as the predicted total dieselization of America's railroad was nearing reality, the railroad industry became disenchanted with the full carbody design used by EMD's Fs and their competition. The operational limitations of single-direction units proved constraining. Furthermore, full carbody designs were not conducive to switching moves, could pose difficulties in the event of a lead locomotive failure on the road, and

EMD's 1,500-horsepower postwar F3 was one of the most popular diesel designs in the mid-1940s. A Monon F3A is seen at 15th Street in Chicago, Illinois. Monon's distinctive paint scheme was designed by Raymond Loewy using Indiana University's school colors.
Richard Jay Solomon

War and Locomotives

The advent of World War II and U.S. involvement had a dramatic short-term effect on railroad traffic and locomotive production. During the years immediately preceding the war, American railroads began to recover the traffic they had lost during the decade-long Depression, but following the Japanese attack on Pearl Harbor in December 1941, freight and passenger traffic soared to unprecedented levels as the nation geared up for war. Never had American railroads experienced such a surge in traffic in such a short time, and they were desperate for motive power, which was suddenly in very short supply. Many lines had not placed significant locomotive orders since before the onset of the Great Depression in 1929, and were operating worn-out steam fleets that were more than 15 years old. Some lines had purchased diesels, but steam still ruled the rails. There were only 1,111 diesels in American service in 1940, so as traffic swelled, locomotive builders were swamped with orders, and every old steam locomotive that had been sitting around idle during the Depression was reactivated and fired up. Some locomotives that had been stricken from the roster and designated as scrap were restored to service. Compounding the locomotive shortage, in April 1942 the War Production Board, a Federal agency set up a few months earlier to oversee the allocation of strategic industrial materials for the war effort, took control of American locomotive production, limiting locomotive construction and allocating locomotive facilities and materials for military purposes.

The War Production Board (WPB) included representatives from the various locomotive builders and significant parts suppliers who assisted in the board's recommendations. Production was divvied up by type in an effort to standardize procurement, and more important, to minimize supply line problems that might be caused by a multitude of incompatible parts. The WPB permitted steam builders to construct steam locomotives that were based on established, tested designs and restricted the number of new designs to be built. Some railroads, such as the Pennsylvania, were forced to accept another railroad's design for the sake of efficiency, rather than pursue its own. Diesel production was severely curtailed because diesels required crucial and scarce materials such as copper used for electrical systems and traction motors, and alloyed steel for engine blocks. Since EMD had developed the only practical road freight locomotive, it was limited to the production of FTs, while Baldwin and Alco diesels were essentially limited to yard switchers (plus Alco's RS-1 road switchers and a few DL109 road locomotives). Although no explicit limitations were placed on the research and development of new locomotive models or new engine types, the builders were not permitted to make any significant changes in production models until the end of the war.

The war had a distinct effect on dieselization. It simultaneously perpetuated the steam locomotive while also creating an enormous demand for diesels after the war because of worn-out steam fleets. The war also enhanced and refined heavy production techniques. If the war had not been a factor in locomotive selection, it is likely that fewer railroads would have ordered steam. An example was the Baltimore & Ohio, which had desired additional EMD FTs but received 2-8-8-4 EM-1s instead. Without the unusual wartime traffic, far fewer new locomotives would have been required. So when restrictions on diesels were lifted, orders flooded the manufacturers, and builders could not supply locomotives fast enough to meet demand. In 1945, with only 2,864 diesels in service, less than 12 percent of the road diesel market potential had been addressed. Fourteen years later, American railroads had achieved total dieselization.

Each builder's market share was also affected by the war. Railroad historian Albert Churella claims that Alco and Baldwin both gained at EMD's expense since EMD was not allowed to construct diesel switchers, the most lucrative segment of the market before the war. During late 1942 and early 1943 EMD's production facilities were focused exclusively on supplying engines for military applications; no EMD diesel locomotives were built during that period. The company lost additional business when potential orders for FTs were denied and instead filled with steam locomotives. Alco, Baldwin, and locomotive newcomer Fairbanks-Morse all developed new diesels during the war to better compete in the postwar market. EMD also improved its existing designs, exhibiting new models immediately after the war. Its FT was supplanted by the more powerful and more reliable F3, and the E7 was introduced as its new passenger locomotive. Perhaps the greatest advantage EMD gained from its war experience was the refinement of its production process. During the war EMD needed to produce diesels as efficiently as possible, and it adopted mass-production techniques while simultaneously expanding its facilities. Before the war it was only capable of building about 40 locomotives a month. By the end of the war it could produce five locomotives a day. Although the postwar environment presented EMD with competition in every locomotive category, it quickly regained market share lost during the war and assumed the role of America's foremost locomotive builder. A few stubborn railroads clung to steam technology for a few more years, refining steam technology to new levels of efficiency and reliability, but for all practical purposes the steam locomotive was dead, and the diesel was the locomotive of the future. Less than 15 years after the end of the war, the steam locomotive was finally vanquished as a mainline revenue hauler, and the diesel had entered its next generation.

In the 1970s Santa Fe's Cleburne, Texas, Shops rebuilt many F7As into CF7 road switchers. In the 1980s Santa Fe disposed of its CF7 fleet, selling it to shortlines. On January 22, 1996, Louisiana & Delta CF7 runs long hood first across the bayou at Delcambre, Louisiana. The L&D is one of several Genesee & Wyoming shortline railroads.

The westbound *California Zephyr* makes a station stop at Denver Union Station in 1966 to pick up passengers and exchange the Burlington E-units that brought the train from Chicago, for Rio Grande F7s. To the right of the *Zephyr* is a Rio Grande EMD SW1200, and a World War II vintage Burlington Alco S-2 switcher featuring Blunt trunks. *Richard Jay Solomon*

required turning facilities if only a single "A" unit was employed. They were also significantly more difficult to maintain than hood unit designs. After 1953, few railroads ordered Fs, and by 1960 EMD had stopped producing them. In a victory of practicality over aesthetics, the clean, streamlined design of the F-unit, with its handsome "bulldog nose" and stylish paint schemes, gave way to the boxy, unrefined, brute look of the road switcher.

By the late 1950s, railroads began replacing their covered wagons with increasingly more powerful hood units. By the early 1970s, the F-unit was an anachronism. A few survived on some lines, often in secondary mainline freight service, but they frequently wore simplified paint schemes that typified a new era of American railroading. The role of the F had gone from standardized common road power to antique curiosity. Some still run today, largely on tourist lines, shortlines, and in museums. A few railroads such as Kansas City Southern, reacquired F-units in the 1990s to use as streamlined power for executive passenger trains, while other lines prefer to use E-units for such duties.

Not all F-units were sent to scrap. A fair number were rebuilt for other applications. In the 1970s, Santa Fe remanufactured its F7s at its Cleburne (Texas) Shops into "CF7" road switchers. The full carbody gave way to a supporting underframe and hood style configuration, but the internal components remained essentially the same. The CF7 bore little resemblance to an F-unit, although some early conversions retained a short section of the F-unit roof line for the locomotive cab. In the early 1980s, Santa Fe sold the majority of its CF7 fleet, mostly to shortlines. During the mid 1970s, Illinois Central Gulf rebuilt a number of aging Gulf Mobile & Ohio F3s and F7s into "FP10" passenger locomotives for Boston's Massachusetts Bay Transportation Authority, where they served for more than a dozen years in push-pull suburban commuter service. Other commuter rail agencies used F-unit locomotives as control cabs in conjunction with push-pull operations. Typically the F-unit power plant was used to provide headend power for heating and lighting, and serve as a cab for the locomotive engineer when the train was in the push mode, but did not have traction motors. This concept required another locomotive to power the train. Other F-units found work as rolling power plants. Southern Pacific converted some F "B" units to power-cars for its mammoth Leslie rotary snowplows used to clear Donner Pass in California and its Cascade crossing in Oregon.

This classic lineup of locomotives at the Cincinnati Union Terminal engine house clearly shows the difference between Electro-Motive's prewar slant nose E-unit and its postwar "bulldog nose" counterparts. From left to right: Louisville & Nashville E7A 791, L&N E6A 771, Pennsylvania E8A 5873, and Cincinnati Union Terminal Lima-Hamilton 750 horsepower switcher No. 20. *Richard Jay Solomon*

On July 22, 1958, a pair of EMD E7s leaves St. Louis leading the Gulf, Mobile & Ohio's *Alton Limited* for Chicago. Behind the train is St. Louis Union Station's vast cantilever train shed, one of the last great train sheds left in North America (although today it no longer serves trains). The E7 was EMD's most popular passenger locomotive and it built more than 500 E7A and E7Bs between 1945 and 1949. Powering the E7 was a pair of EMD's successful 12-cylinder 567A engines. *Richard Jay Solomon*

EMD FL9

Among the most unusual diesel-electrics in America were New Haven's 60 FL9s—dual-mode F-units specifically designed to operate into New York's electrified Grand Central Terminal and Pennsylvania Station, and its river tunnels using lineside third rail DC power. For many years the FL9s were the only diesel-electric/electric locomotives in North America (see GENESIS sidebar). The FL9 was EMD's economical solution to New Haven's complex motive power quandary. In the mid-1950s, the financially strapped New Haven was faced with a unique situation. Its aging electric fleet, some dating back to the original 1905 electrification, desperately needed replacement, as did its fleet of World War II-vintage Alco DL109s. Railroad management wanted to dieselize portions of its 50-year-old electrification and focus electric operations on New York—Stamford suburban runs. It wanted to eliminate expensive, time-consuming engine changes at New Haven and Danbury. However, it could not simply buy commercially produced 'off-the-shelf' diesels for the run into New York City because of strict anti-pollution regulations. New Haven entertained a proposal to rebuild the DL109s into dual-mode locomotives, but rejected it largely because they would have been too heavy for safe operations on the Park Avenue Viaduct in Manhattan (which had unusually strict weight restrictions).

The FL9 solved most of New Haven's problems: using a lengthened FP9 carbody, EMD built a diesel-electric passenger locomotive capable of operating from a 660-volt DC third rail, as well as from its own 567 engine and generator. The FL9 was equipped with special third rail shoes that could operate on both New York Central's underrunning third rail, as well as Pennsylvania's overrunning third rail. To accommodate low axle loadings on the Park Avenue viaduct, EMD used an A1A flexicoil truck to support the rear of the locomotive, thus distributing the weight over five axles instead of four. As a result, the FL9 was one of only a few locomotives to employ a B-A1A wheel arrangement. According to *Diesels to Park Avenue* by Joe Snopek and Robert A. La May, the "L" in the FL9 designation indicates "lengthened," although other sources suggest that it stands for "<u>e</u>lectric."

A pair of brand-new EMD FL9s leading a train from Boston roll through New York Central's Mott Haven Yard in The Bronx, while a NYC Alco S-3 switcher waits on an adjacent track. Richard Jay Solomon

The first order of 30 FL9s, supplied between 1956 and 1957, used the 567C diesel engine, which delivered 1,750 horsepower. New Haven required more FL9s but could not afford them until 1960, when it took delivery of another 30 units. The second group was slightly different from the first. They were powered by the 567D1, which generated 1,800 horsepower. All the locomotives were dressed in the flashy red, white, and black paint scheme first used on New Haven's ten EP-5 electrics. The FL9 had a noticeable effect on New Haven's operations, replacing several older classes of electrics and the DL109s, and minimizing the railroad's reliance on other types of passenger power.

Following New Haven's inclusion in the Penn-Central in 1969, and the creation of Amtrak in 1971, the FL9 fleet assumed new duties. While New Haven had operated the majority of its Boston-to-New York runs into Grand Central, Amtrak preferred the Penn Station routing via the Hell Gate Bridge, and most corridor trains were now operated through from Boston to Washington, D. C. This eliminated the need for FL9s on the Boston trains, and many were reassigned to suburban trains on the former New York Central Hudson and Harlem lines, while others remained on the former New Haven's Danbury to Grand Central runs. Some FL9s were assigned to Amtrak, and worked on Empire Corridor trains, allowing trains from Albany and Buffalo to operate directly into Grand Central without an engine change at Croton-Harmon, New York (see GENESIS sidebar). The FL9 survived into the late 1990s, primarily as a suburban commuter locomotive operated by Metro North—the railroad responsible for suburban service out of Grand Central. Over the years the FL9s have been rebuilt and modified several times. They were the last EMD F-units built for domestic use, and the last large active fleet of Fs operating in the United States.

FL9 Statistics:
Builder: EMD
Engine: 16-cylinder 567C/567D1
Horsepower: 1,750/1,800

Wheel Arrangement: B-A1A
Length: 58 feet, 8 inches
Total built: 60

Chicago is America's railroad capital, and no American city has more railroads or railroad activity. In the 1950s there would have been no better place to see new diesels in action than Chicago on a sunny day. Shortly after noon, on July 21, 1958, Richard Jay Solomon photographed a remarkable three-way-convergence near 16th street: Wabash E8A No. 1000 rolls beneath a New York Central E7A/E8A pair, as two Rock Island Alco RS-3s and a EMD F, wait in a yard on the left. *Richard Jay Solomon*

Postwar E's

Following World War II, Electro-Motive introduced its E7, a mass-produced 2,000-horsepower passenger diesel. It shared some qualities with prewar models but featured greater reliability than earlier Es. It looked slightly different, featuring the rounded "bulldog" nose, instead of the steeply slanted nose used on prewar Es. The E7A measured 71 feet, 1.25 inches long, while the E7B was about a foot shorter. The locomotive was in production for four years beginning in 1945, and became one of the most popular passenger locomotives ever designed: 428 E7As were built and 82 E7Bs. In 1949, the E8 superseded the E7, coincident with similar model upgrades in the Electro-Motive catalog. The E8 was slightly more powerful, delivering 2,250 horsepower and incorporating a variety of incremental improvements (such as electric cooling fans). It was the first EMD E to offer a dynamic braking option. Electro-Motive sold 421 E8As in the United States and Canada between 1949 and 1955, when it was superseded by the 2,400-horsepower E9. By this time the passenger locomotive market had declined dramatically.

During the 1940s and early 1950s, railroads were quick to replace Pacific, Hudson, and Northern-type steam locomotives typically used on passenger trains with new, cleaner diesels. Flagship passenger trains were often the first main-line runs to regularly receive diesel power. As a result many lines had effectively eliminated their passenger steam by 1953, resulting in a comparatively small market for new passenger locomotives. Furthermore, by the mid-1950s American railroads were suffering from a dramatic loss of passengers as people embraced the automobile with renewed fervor. Commercial airlines with improved propeller aircraft, and later jet planes, decimated long-distance train travel.

While some railroads continued to introduce new streamlined trains and attempted to improve services, passenger revenues spiraled downward until the early 1970s, when the federal government created Amtrak to assume remaining intercity passenger operations. As ridership dropped, railroads trimmed services and eliminated trains—a poor market for new passenger locomotives. So, while the E9 remained in production until 1964, longer than the combined runs of the E7 and E8, only 100 E9As and 44 E9Bs were built.

During its three-decade production run, Electro-Motive's E-unit became the standard long-distance passenger locomotive. E-units hauled everything from Southern Pacific's *Coast Daylight* and famous *Sunset Limited* to Pennsylvania's

continued on page 70

Following page
Although EMD E-units were designed for passenger work, in later years, following the discontinuation of many passenger trains, some lines assigned them to freight service. On January 21, 1973, Erie Lackawanna E8A 817 leads an eastbound freight along the Canisteo River near Cameron Mills, New York. *Doug Eisele*

EMD SD7

EMD entered the six-axle, six-motor road-switcher market in 1951, with the introduction of its Special Duty line, the SD7, following the lead of Baldwin, which had been selling six-motor road switchers since the late 1940s. The SD7 was essentially a six-motor version of EMD's pioneer four-axle road switcher, the GP7. Like its four-axle counterpart, the SD7 featured a 16-cylinder 567B engine, which generated 1,500 horsepower. In most respects it resembled the GP7, but it was nearly five feet longer, featured six-axle hi-adhesion Flexicoil trucks, and distinctive large radiators at the rear of the hood. The Flexicoil truck permitted easy access to the center traction motor, an important consideration for maintenance crews. (A decade earlier, Alco had used six-axle trucks on some of its RS-1 exports and military locomotives that suffered from restrictive access to the center traction motor. As a result, Alco needed to redesign its six-axle truck before introducing it to the domestic market.) The SD7 was capable of negotiating 23-degree curves, ascending grades as steep as 5 percent, hauling a 5,500-ton train in level territory, or a 1,500-ton train over a 2 percent grade. Like most road switchers, it was versatile and intended to handle a variety of tasks, from moving suburban passenger runs to heavy freight trains and yard work.

EMD's SD7 demonstrator was smartly adorned in bright red paint and toured over prospective railroads. One of the first buyers, and ultimately EMD's largest SD7 customer, was Southern Pacific, which had purchased a fair number of Baldwin's six-motor locomotives. Southern Pacific's rugged profile was natural six-motor territory. Steep grades and heavy tonnage required lots of tractive effort.

Southern Pacific was one of the last railroads to operate SD7s, and several survived in yard service until SP was merged into Union Pacific in 1996. In November 1989, SP SD7 1528 rolls along on the mainline near Sacramento, California.

However, one of the first assignments for the SD7 was on SP's Northwestern Pacific subsidiary, which ran between the Bay Area and Eureka, California. While the NWP featured some formidable stretches of three percent grade, the primary reason for SP assigning six-motor locomotives on this route was to minimize damage to bridges and track through reduced axle loadings, another major advantage of a six-axle locomotive. Southern Pacific ultimately acquired 43 of the 188 SD7s built. SP also acquired large numbers of SD9s, EMD's 1,750 horsepower successor to the SD7. In the late 1970s and early 1980s, SP rebuilt many of its older 567-powered locomotives, including the SD7s. This rebuilding extended the SD7's life by nearly two decades, and some SD7s lasted to the very end of SP's independent operations when SP was absorbed by western giant Union Pacific.

Among other SD7 buyers were Baltimore & Ohio, Bessemer & Lake Erie, Burlington, Chicago & North Western, Erie, Great Northern, Milwaukee Road, Pennsylvania Railroad, and Union Pacific. The SD7 was the first of what would ultimately become EMD's most successful type of locomotive. By the mid-1960s six-motor locomotives were outselling four-motor locomotives, and by the mid-1990s few railroads were ordering anything but six-motor locomotives. Yet in 1951 the six-motor locomotive was a specialty item.

SD7 Statistics:
Builder: EMD
Engine: 16-cylinder 567B
Horsepower: 1,500

Wheel Arrangement: C-C
Length: 60 feet, 9 inches
Total built: 188

continued from page 67

EMD's first attempt at building a road switcher was its BL1/BL2 branchline locomotive, which was essentially an F3 with a different style carbody. The Rock Island was one of several lines to purchase BL2s, and often used them in Chicago area commuter service. Offering a good comparison of the carbody styles, Rock Island BL2 425 and FP7A 410 rest nose to nose at Blue Island, Illinois.
Richard Jay Solomon

Broadway Limited and New York Central's renowned *Twentieth Century Limited*, a fact that made Electro-Motive's Dick Dilworth, the locomotive's principal designer, especially proud. Ironically, the E-unit that was born in an effort to attract renewed interest in passenger trains also became the locomotive that hauled many final runs. By the late 1960s, the faded, worn E-unit hauling a short, lightly patronized train of just a coach or two, became a symbol of the passenger train's sad decline.

"Branch line Locomotive"

Other manufacturers offered road-switchers, but EMD was slow to embrace this popular type. Since EMD had captured the majority of the road diesel market, and had

no difficulty selling locomotives, it was not compelled to design a new type that might simply compete with its existing designs. EMD was initially content to focus its production on the three basic types it felt would generate the most profit: switchers, Es, and Fs. However, by the late 1940s, it was willing to develop the road-switcher market, and its first attempt was the distinctive-looking, semi-streamlined, BL1/BL2 "Branchline locomotive," developed in 1947 and introduced in 1948. The BL2 combined features of an F-unit with some of the convenience of a road-switcher. Provided with a bidirectional view, the engineer could easily operate the engine in either direction; foot boards aided in switching moves. Initially BL2s were not built for multiple-unit operation, but EMD soon rectified this deficiency. These curious looking machines did not sell well compared to the Fs. Only 59 were built, and production ended after a little more than a year. It

A pair of Chicago & North Western GP7s pass through Johnson Creek, Wisconsin, on their way from Jefferson Junction to a connection with C&NW's Milwaukee—Twin Cities, "Adams Line" at Clyman Junction. Although these locomotives were originally owned by Rock Island, they were later part of C&NW's pioneering GP7 fleet. C&NW bought the very first GP7 in October 1949.

Duluth, Missabe & Iron Range maintained one of the largest fleets of EMD SD9s. When they were new, these 1,750-horsepower, six-motor locomotives were ideally suited for high-tractive effort applications and were purchased by DM&IR to haul exceptionally heavy ore trains from the Iron Range to docks on Lake Superior at Duluth and Two Harbors, Minnesota. On September 25, 1994, DM&IR SD9 166, still its original paint scheme, rolls toward Proctor, Minnesota, with a loaded taconite train.

By April 1995, C&NW GP7 4141 had a long history going back more than 40 years, during which it carried at least four different road numbers. It was built by EMD for Rock Island in 1952, then rebuilt by Rock's Silvis, Illinois, shops in 1976 before being sold to C&NW. In the spring of 1995 it became part of Union Pacific's fleet, when C&NW merged with UP. When this GP7 was new, steam locomotives were still common. By 1995, new AC traction diesels were taking hold.

was an interesting first step into what would develop as EMD's most lucrative market.

Soon after it discontinued the BL2, EMD introduced a true road switcher.

General Purpose

The GP7, a 1,500-horsepower road switcher in a hood configuration, was introduced in 1949, just ten years after the FT made its debut. This stark-looking utilitarian machine embraced most of the same components as the F7, introduced at about the same time. The versatility and reliability of the GP7, combined with an ease of maintenance facilitated by its simple hood design, made the model an instant success. By the early 1950s the hood-style road switcher had become EMD's fastest-selling locomotive. In a production run that lasted just five years, EMD built more than 2,700 GP7s, and this model alone accounted for almost 10 percent of the American locomotive fleet at the close of the steam era. EMD expanded its GP7 into a six-axle, six-motor design in 1952 (see SD7 sidebar).

In 1954, EMD introduced the 1,750-horsepower GP9, along with its higher horsepower F9, SD9, and E9. The GP9

outsold even the GP7, and in less than six years EMD had built more than 3,500 GP9s for domestic use. Ultimately, more than 4,000 GP9s were built for North American service, including some cabless GP9Bs for Union Pacific and the Pennsylvania Railroad.

The GP represented a vast improvement over most earlier diesels. It gave EMD an even greater advantage over other locomotive builders, allowing it to secure an even larger share of the new locomotive market, which it already dominated by the late 1940s. The GP also spelled doom for most remaining steam operations. Some railroads that had resisted dieselization, such as the Norfolk & Western, changed their mind when they concluded that the improved performance of GPs outweighed any financial advantages offered by steam power. Norfolk & Western had been the last major railroad to use steam on a large scale, one of a few railroads to manufacture a large portion of its motive power, and as late as 1953 it was still building new steam switchers. But with the introduction of the GP9, N & W stopped building steam locomotives, and within just six years, it dumped the ashes for the last time.

In 1959, EMD introduced the 1,800-horsepower GP18 in place of the GP9 for the American market

Opposite: EMD's GP9s had a long, productive career on Southern Pacific and many were rebuilt as GP9Es by SP's Sacramento and Houston shops in the 1970s. On April 18, 1993, five GP9Es roar past Pinole, California, along the shore of San Pablo Bay.

The diesel-electric afforded cost savings that may have spared many lines from total insolvency. On August 21, 1994, a Wisconsin & Southern GP9 rolls west toward Prairie du Chien, Wisconsin.

(GMD, EMD's Canadian subsidiary, continued to build GP9s for the Canadian market until 1963). This locomotive represented a nominal improvement over the GP9, and used a 16-cylinder 567D1 engine that generated 1,800 horsepower. A more significant improvement to EMD's locomotive line, however, was its 2,000-horsepower GP20, its first locomotive to employ a supercharger to obtain greater power output. The GP20, and its six-motor counterpart, the SD24, led to a whole new line of EMD diesels, and marked a change in the locomotive market. EMD, which until this time had only embraced nominal increases in horsepower, now aimed to build significantly more powerful locomotives. Many locomotive historians mark this technological change, combined with other market forces such as the effect of total dieselization, as the dividing line between first generation and second generation diesels. The push to replace steam with reliable diesel-electrics had been successful, and now railroads had whole fleets of aging diesels that needed upgrading, rebuilding, or replacing.

4

ALCO

"STEAM HAS BEEN THE PRINCIPAL RAILROAD MOTIVE POWER.
IT STILL IS, [AND] IN MY VIEW WILL CONTINUE TO BE."

—*From an address by Alco president William C. Dickerman
in 1938, quoted in Albert Churella's* From Steam to Diesel.

DURING THE EARLY YEARS of commercial diesel production, the American Locomotive Company, better known as Alco, was among the foremost diesel producers in the United States, in second place behind EMD in sales and reliability. Alco was firmly established as a steam builder when it joined with General Electric and Ingersoll Rand in the construction of pioneering CNJ 1000 in 1925. By the late 1920s, Alco could see the value of building diesel switchers, and left the GE-IR consortium to pursue its own diesel designs. In 1929, Alco acquired a majority share in McIntosh & Seymore in order to advance its diesel engine design for practical locomotive application. Within two years two engines were developed for use in locomotives, and Alco began building commercial diesel-electric switchers. One was a 300-horsepower engine that was only applied to a

handful of early switchers; the other was a more successful design that generated 600 horsepower. This engine, designated 531 (Alco engine designations typically use the last two digits to indicate the year a model entered production), was a 12.5x13-inch inline six-cylinder, four-cycle diesel that operated at 700 rpm and generated 600 horsepower. Its basic design was modified in 1938, becoming the 538 engine, and again in 1939 as the 539 engine. Essentially this same engine remained in production until the early 1960s, long after Alco had developed more-powerful designs.

Prior to 1936 Alco built more than 30 diesel switchers for commercial purposes. A few used a boxcab design that resembled other diesels of the period, but most employed a hood design inspired by the Westinghouse "visibility cab." In 1934 Alco hired noted industrial designer Otto Kuhler to

Two classic locomotives side by side: Pennsylvania's GG1 electric, a design refined by Raymond Loewy, and an Alco PA. Many consider the Alco PA the best-looking diesel-electric ever built. On May 10, 1959, near Newark, New Jersey, PRR and LV exchange locomotives for one of Lehigh's westbound passenger trains, the *John Wilkes*. Lehigh Valley long-distance passenger trains began serving PRR's Penn Station during World War I. *Richard Jay Solomon*

improve the appearance of its 600-horsepower switcher. Kuhler's treatment of the switcher was minimal yet distinctive, unlike his elaborate streamlining designs. He raised the hood level to match the roof line of the cab, recessed headlights, and made other minor aesthetic improvements. These locomotives used the distinctive "Blunt" truck named for its designer.

In 1936, Alco began building 660-horsepower and 900-horsepower switchers that conformed with new industry diesel standards. Although Alco did not apply model designations to its diesels in this formative period, these locomotives are known colloquially as High Hood switchers, and often receive HH660 and HH900 (and later HH1000) designations

from locomotive chroniclers to distinguish their hood style and power from later models.

In its early years of diesel production, Alco employed electrical gear from both General Electric and Westinghouse, but by 1940 Alco agreed to use General Electric as its sole electrical supplier, and the two companies entered a formal production agreement that lasted until the early 1950s.

In 1937, Alco became the first diesel builder to apply a turbocharger to a railroad engine in order to boost output. A turbocharger increases output by increasing fuel combustion using a turbine to force air into the cylinder. Alco's 1,000-horsepower turbocharged engine was designated 531T. Turbochargers later became a standard tool

The Jay Street Connecting Railroad operated a variety of historically significant diesels. No. 5 is an early Alco switcher, and No. 300 is Alco's first production diesel and the only boxcab switcher it built after leaving the Alco-GE-IR consortium. *Richard Jay Solomon*

for boosting power and are found on all modern high-horsepower locomotives.

S-1 and S-2

The development of the 539 engine resulted in a change in the frame mounting, permitting Alco to lower the hood on its switchers, which allowed better visibility. In 1940, Alco introduced its 660 horsepower S-1 and 1,000 horsepower S-2 switchers with lower hoods and the recently introduced 539 engine. The S-2 obtained its additional 340 horsepower through turbocharging. Both locomotives used the Blunt truck design employed on early Alco switchers. These two switchers were among Alco's most popular diesel designs, remaining in production for ten years. The company sold more than 2,000 of them to American railroads. While to the casual observer both locomotives looked nearly identical, the turbocharged 1,000-horsepower S-2 was nearly three times more common than the S-1. Alco switchers were found in switching service everywhere, toiling away in obscurity on menial duties from shuttling passenger cars to the coach yard, to working industrial trackage along city streets and back alleys. They were hardly noticed by diesel watchers and enthusiasts until they had nearly vanished from the railroad scene.

Shortly after the introduction of its S-unit switchers, Alco brought out an expanded locomotive design for both switching and road work. Its RS-1 is generally regarded as the first successful mass-produced roadswitcher (see Alco RS-1 sidebar).

Early Alco Road Locomotives

Throughout the 1930s, switchers were the primary market for diesels, representing by far the largest segment of production. However, Electro-Motive's successful E-unit prompted Alco to design its own high-horsepower road locomotive. Research began in 1938, and in 1940 Alco demonstrated a 2,000-horsepower, streamlined, full carbody locomotive riding on a pair of A1A trucks. Its slanted knifelike nose and three-piece windshield displayed Otto Kuhler's trademark styling; it was unlikely to be mistaken for an Electro-Motive product. Two turbocharged 538T engines powered a prototype that was sold to the Rock Island. Alco intended the locomotive for dual service and offered a variety of gear ratios that would allow for top speeds ranging from 80 to 120 miles per hour. Production locomotives, specification numbers DL109 (cabs) and DL110 (boosters), measured 74 feet, 6.5 inches, and 72 feet, 4 inches, respectively (slightly shorter than the prototype), and employed the new 539T engine, rated the same as the 538T.

Some of the early locomotives were retroactively assigned different specifications, causing some confusion. The prototype is often described as a DL103b, while the first two production locomotives are described as DL105s, and the

next two DL107s. Differences between these locomotives are minor, and Alco did not assign them model designations. Alco was permitted to build some DL109s during World War II, despite strict War Production Board restrictions limiting road diesel allocation. The last DL109s were built in 1945, by which time Alco had created more advanced designs, which it built following the war.

While there was nominal interest in Alco's road diesel, railroad response was unimpressive. New Haven displayed the most enthusiasm, purchasing a fleet of 60 DL109s—most of the production run. They were painted in an attractive dark green and yellow—similar to New Haven's electrics. The DL109s were New Haven's first road diesels and they were assigned to dual service, typically on passenger trains during the day and on freight at night.

Alco Abandons Steam

Although Alco had geared up to build diesel switchers and attempted to compete in the road-diesel market with its DL109/DL110, the vast majority of its locomotive business in the late 1930s and early 1940s was filling conventional reciprocating steam locomotive orders. Alco had been responsible for many of the best known and most influential steam designs in the United States. In 1904, it had built the first American Mallet Compound for the Baltimore & Ohio, a type that quickly became popular as a slow-speed mountain locomotive. In the 1920s, Alco worked with New York

Alco's prewar competition to the Electro-Motive E-unit was its DL 100 series cabs, featuring a carbody styled by Otto Kuhler. Rock Island DL107 No. 622 leads the Jet Rocket westbound through Blue Island, Illinois, in the summer of 1958. *Richard Jay Solomon*

Central in developing that railroad's legendary 4-6-4 Hudson type. Later it built Central's 4-8-2 Mohawks, and in the mid-1940s was working with Central to expand on these successful designs to produce one of the best performing steam locomotives ever to roll on American rails, New York Central's 4-8-4 Niagara. Alco built Union Pacific's 4-6-6-4 Challengers, and went on to build UP's famous 4-8-8-4 Big Boys—among the largest locomotives ever constructed. In 1935, when Milwaukee Road wanted to operate high-speed streamlined passenger trains at more than 100 miles per hour, it turned to Alco—not for slick, diesel-powered articulated trains, but for fast steam power. Alco fulfilled Milwaukee's request, first with shrouded 4-4-2 Atlantics—the first new streamlined steam in America—then with larger streamlined 4-6-4 Hudsons.

With this impressive lineup of locomotive designs, and a long legacy of steam power behind them, it was difficult for Alco to reconcile the fact that the mainstay of its business had no future. Certainly the diesel had made a good showing, Alco executives realized, but that did not necessarily mean that steam would entirely disappear. Alco envisioned a gradual transition in its product line as diesels became more dominant.

World War II must have reinforced this thinking, because while Alco was swamped with orders for military equipment—it supplied more than 7,000 tanks and other machinery—it was building more steam locomotives than it had since before the onset of the Great Depression. It built more than a thousand steam locomotives during the war and only 157 diesels. As the war was drawing to a close, Alco anticipated a great need for new locomotives, both steam and diesel. In 1946 some railroads were still ordering new steam locomotives, and a large portion of Alco's locomotive business was in steam. By 1947 the domestic steam business had dropped off dramatically as orders for new diesels poured in, yet Alco management was slow to respond to this drastic change in motive power demand. Albert Churella notes that in 1947 an Alco official optimistically stated, "We do not, by any means, believe the steam locomotive is dead." A year later that official may have believed otherwise: after completing an order for Pittsburgh & Lake Erie 2-8-4 Berkshires, Alco ceased steam locomotive production.

Although Alco may have had faith in the longevity of the steam locomotive, it also responded to the rapidly expanding diesel market, and tried to stay abreast of developments in order to remain competitive. It has been argued that if Alco had not been so preoccupied with traditional steam locomotive building, and conventional building practices, the company may have been in a better position to compete with the nation's foremost diesel builder, EMD. During the war Alco furthered its diesel research and development preparing for postwar diesel sales, but did so less effectively than EMD, and suffered as a result. This trend was neither obvious to industry observers nor to Alco at the time. During the war years Alco nearly doubled its market share of diesel production. According to Churella, in 1941 Alco commanded just 21 percent of the diesel market but by 1946 it had roughly 40 percent. The years following the war, however, were extremely competitive in the diesel marketplace, and while Alco maintained its position as the number two diesel builder, it gradually lost market share to EMD.

Alco's losses have been attributed to a multitude of causes. Churella believes the company suffered from a steam locomotive mentality, building locomotives in small numbers to meet customer needs instead of embracing EMD's automotivelike mass production techniques. This raised Alco's per-unit engineering costs and tended to reduce locomotive reliability. Another problem was labor related: Alco employees were better compensated than EMD's, resulting in much higher labor costs. Following the war, Alco was plagued by strikes that resulted in lost production and a damaged reputation. But one of its biggest problems lay in locomotive reliability. While Alco locomotives generally performed well, and often had higher horsepower ratings than their EMD counterparts, many railroads felt that Alco's machines required more attention and incurred significantly higher maintenance costs than EMD's. Alco tried to match the competition by making modifications to its locomotives, yet while it improved designs, incrementally raising horsepower, tractive effort output, and reliability, Alco still lost market share as the total dieselization of American railroads became a reality during the 1950s. By 1953 it held just 15 percent of the market and was finding it had fewer and fewer repeat customers.

Unwilling to accept blame for its declining market share, during the 1950s and 1960s the company blamed the War Production Board and EMD for its woes. These allegations proved misguided. Although many larger roads tended to favor EMD, Alco survived through the 1950s as the nation's second-largest locomotive producer. After Baldwin and Fairbanks-Morse exited the business, it would have been imprudent of the railroads to allow EMD to assume 100 percent of American locomotive production, so Alco typically received small orders from most major carriers that kept it in the locomotive business. A number of smaller, middle-sized railroads that had always bought Alco locomotives remained loyal to the traditional builder, well after EMD had demonstrated a superior locomotive design. Lines such as the Delaware & Hudson, Lehigh Valley, Green Bay & Western, and Spokane, Portland & Seattle remained Alco railroads as long as the company sold locomotives.

In the early 1950s, GE dissolved its partnership with Alco, but Alco continued to employ GE electrical gear. This move was General Electric's first step toward entering the American heavy locomotive market, a move that would ultimately prove disastrous for Alco. In the mid-1950s, Alco changed its company name from the American Locomotive

Company to Alco Products, reflecting the company's attempt to diversify into other fields. Through the 1950s, Alco updated its designs and implemented a variety of improvements, including a new, more reliable, and more powerful engine.

In the early 1960s, despite new competition from its one-time partner, GE, Alco made a significant investment in locomotive development by introducing its new Century line (see Chapter 7).

Wartime Development

Although the WPB restricted the production of new locomotive designs, there were no specific prohibitions against developmental efforts. Alco initially focused its efforts on the development of its 241 diesel engine, an entirely new four-cycle engine design intended for use in road locomotives. It used a 9x10.5-inch bore and stroke, which, in its 12-cylinder application, was designed to provide 1,500 horsepower—a dramatic improvement over the six-cylinder 12.5x13-inch 539 design. Despite roughly three years of work and varying amounts of interest by Alco engineers, the engine design was dropped and never entered regular production. Instead Alco decided to develop the 244 engine based on elements of the 241 design: both engines used the same 9x10.5-inch configuration, and had roughly the same output. During the war

Alco also refined its 539 design used in its switchers, and tried to develop an opposed piston engine to rival the Fairbanks-Morse design, without success.

In 1943 Alco began work on a four-axle carbody road locomotive to compete with EMD's FT. This work resulted in the September 1945 debut of a streamlined A-B-A locomotive rated at 4,500 horsepower, which bore a striking family resemblance to the DL109. Each unit featured B-B trucks, like the FTs. The A-units measured 51 feet, 6 inches, making them roughly 23 feet shorter than the DL109. It's interesting that all were powered by Alco's 241 engine (rated at 1,500 horsepower), although the more successful 244 design was only a few months away from regular production. While the locomotive carried a specification number designation DL203-1 for the A-unit, and DL203-2 B-unit, the locomotive was universally known by its somber nickname, "Black Maria" (pronounced with a long "i"), which reflected its uniform black paint and a near total lack of lettering. Perhaps the name was prophetic, for Black Maria also means hearse, and these locomotives did not survive long. They tested on the Delaware & Hudson, and later performed extensive tests on the New Haven, where they were operated both as a set and as separate units. Toward the end of their short career they went to Maine and tested on the Bangor & Aroostook.

A rare photograph of Alco's Black Maria testing on the New Haven Railroad at Canaan, Connecticut. The train is en route from Pittsfield, Massachusetts, to Danbury, Connecticut. *Tim Doherty collection*

Erie-Lackawanna FA-1 No. 7321 rolls across a weed-grown diamond crossing in the vicinity of Campbell Hall, New York, in the early 1960s, shortly after the Erie and Lackawanna merged. *Richard Jay Solomon*

The Black Maria served more as a prototype than as a railroad demonstrator. Only months after the Black Maria began testing, Alco introduced its successful FA/FB freight full-carbody locomotives.

Postwar Locomotive Designs

In 1946, Alco prepared for the much-anticipated postwar boom in locomotive sales. Alco hoped steam would be a large part of this market, but it also geared up for diesel production and offered several competitive new models.

Alco's FA-1/FB-1 (cab/booster) was designed as competition to EMD's FT four-axle freight locomotive. It was introduced in January 1946 and incorporated much of the Black Maria design, but instead of the 241 engine it used the new 12-cylinder 244 engine aspirated with a GE RD1 turbocharger, and featured an entirely different carbody style. The FA-1 was the first locomotive to feature Alco's distinctive flat nose with a metal grille surrounding the headlight, a design attributed to Ray Patten. The first FA-1s had a fully recessed headlight and grille, which gave the nose a more rounded appearance. On later locomotives, the headlight casing sat a little higher and protruded, interrupting the

Two sets of Alco FA-2s rest at New York Central's former West Shore Yards in North Bergen, New Jersey, on April 13, 1958. New York Central was one of Alco's most loyal customers and operated the largest roster of Alco diesel-electrics in the United States. It had 80 FA-2s and 50 FB-2s, in addition to a sizable fleet of FA/FB-1s. New York Central concentrated its Alco power east of Cleveland, and the FA/FB cabs were typical power on the old West Shore line. *Richard Jay Solomon*

clean nose line and giving the locomotive a more businesslike appearance.

The FA-1/FB-1s were rated at 1,500 horsepower each, and produced a maximum 34,000 pounds continuous tractive effort at 13.5 miles per hour. The FA-1s were 51 feet, 6 inches long—the same length as the Black Maria. The FA-1/FB-1 model designation was retroactively applied to these locomotives in the early 1950s. At the time they were introduced, they were known by their specification numbers, DL208/DL209, but Alco altered the specification numbers by adding a letter suffix as it implemented various design improvements. Similar to EMD's FTs, initially the FA-1/FB-1 employed belt and mechanical drives for various auxiliary rotating appliances, but later FA/FB locomotives employed more practical and reliable auxiliary motors instead, an improvement consistent with industry trends. Maximum continuous tractive effort was increased to 42,500 pounds at 11 miles per hour.

In contrast to its full-carbody FA/FB, Alco also introduced a more powerful road-switcher to supplement the successful 1,000 RS-1 design. Designated RS-2, it was an attractively styled hood locomotive largely based on the RS-1

An Alco FA cab leads a southbound New York Central freight along the West Shore line near Thompsons Cove, New York. In the background are mothballed "Liberty ships" from World War II, stored in the event of a Cold War emergency.
Richard Jay Solomon

Alco's RSC-2 rode on A1A trucks (center axle is unpowered) to reduce axle-loadings for use on lightly built branch lines; they were the same as the four-axle RS-2 in most other respects. In 1946 Milwaukee Road was the first line to order RSC-2s. This locomotive is preserved at the Mid-Continent Railway Museum in North Freedom, Wisconsin.

Alco RS-1

The RS-1 was developed by Alco in 1941 at the request of the Rock Island, which was looking for a branchline locomotive capable of handling a variety of tasks. Rock Island's intent was to reduce branchline expenses by eliminating steam locomotives. The RS-1 (it did not carry that designation until much later) was basically a 1,000-horsepower switcher on a longer frame, which allowed for a short hood that could house a boiler for steam heat. Many authorities concur that the RS-1 was the first true diesel-electric road switcher, a type that would become extremely popular in later years.

The RS-1 was ideal for branchline service. It had twice the availability of the typical branchline steam locomotive, allowing each diesel to replace two steam locomotives. John Kirkland indicates that RS-1 fuel costs were about 1/7th that of steam, and the diesel required fewer men to operate and maintain it, providing the railroad with added savings. Unlike earlier diesels that were designed to handle a specific task, such as switching, long-distance passenger runs, or heavy freight runs, the RS-1 demonstrated remarkable versatility and could adeptly handle passenger, freight, and switching assignments equally well. Like the switcher it was based on, the RS-1 generated 1,000 horsepower using a six-cylinder 539T engine, and it was capable of 60 miles per hour. Although the locomotive remained in domestic production until 1951, and export production until 1960, it continued to use the same prime mover, even after more modern engine designs were introduced.

The RS-1 was developed immediately prior to the United States' involvement in World War II, and the U.S. Army found the new locomotive type especially well suited to military applications. Consequently, it ordered many for work overseas. The majority of these

Livonia, Avon & Lakeville operates a short section of former Erie Railroad in western New York. In September 1986, Alco RS-1 No. 20 leads a short freight into Avon from Lakeville.

locomotives used six-axle trucks rather than the four-axle trucks applied to civilian locomotives. Alco also built an export model of the RS-1 that used A1A trucks to achieve lighter axle loadings. While some diesel writers have retroactively applied the RSD-1 and RSC-1 model designations to these locomotives, diesel historian John Kirkland states that Alco made no such distinction in the model designation. The locomotive variations were all model RS-1 but carried different specification numbers: E1640, E1641, and E1641A for the B-B locomotives; E1645, E1646, and E1647 for the C-Cs; and E1651 for the A1A-A1As. A total of 623 RS-1s were built.

The RS-1 could be found on many American railroads, large and small, performing a variety of secondary duties. While it was unlikely an RS-1 would be out on the mainline hauling a heavy through freight, or leading a luxury limited, it could be found switching in the coach yard, working industrial trackage and branchlines, hauling a milk train or back country mixed train, and working light suburban trains. The RS-1 proved one of Alco's most enduring products, and in the late 1990s some RS-1s were still operating, their 539T prime movers still working hard, long after most of Alco's 1960s–era Century line had gone to the scrapper.

RS-1 Statistics:
Builder: Alco-GE
Engine: Alco six-cylinder 539
Horsepower: 1,000
Wheel Arrangement: B-B/C-C/A1A-A1A
Length: 56 feet
Total built (including exports and six-axle models): 623

design but with the new 244 12-cylinder 1,500-horsepower engine. It had a B-B wheel arrangement, was 55 feet, 11.75 inches long, and weighed about 240,000 pounds Alco also offered an RSC-2 designed for use on lightweight lines. The RSC-2 was built to roughly the same specifications as the RS-2, but with an A1A—A1A wheel arrangement to distribute its weight over six axles to yield lower axle loadings than typical road locomotives. Maximum tractive effort was reduced by about a third as a result of less weight on the drive wheels. Since the cost of power was effectively higher with RSC-2, and it was intended essentially as a specialty locomotive, its sales potential was limited. Domestically, Alco sold 383 RS-2s, but only 70 RSC-2s. Although Alco upgraded the A1A road-switcher design to an RSC-3 in 1950, it opted to discontinue this line a year later, having sold only 19 in the United States and Canada. In the early 1950s changes in the American rate structure for freight billing threatened to cut the already small domestic market for light road locomotives, although the Canadian and export markets supported a number of light locomotive designs.

Alco's postwar successor to the DL109 was its remarkably handsome PA model, a 2,000-horsepower streamlined passenger locomotive riding on A1A trucks. The PA shared a family resemblance with the FA locomotive, but featured a pronounced 6-foot-long nose (see Alco PA sidebar).

Alco Upgrades

In 1950 Alco boosted the output of its 244 engine to 1,600 horsepower, to make its locomotives more competitive with EMD F7s. Later that year Alco introduced new model designations that reflected a variety of technological improvements, although these new models did not specifically reflect horsepower increases. Alco's model upgrades were coincident with new models introduced by Baldwin and F-M that also incorporated power increases from 1,500 horsepower to 1,600 horsepower. General Motors, which dominated the market, selling far more locomotives than the other three builders put together, did not follow this trend, and continued to build 1,500-horsepower locomotives as its standard models until January 1954.

Among Alco's new models were FA-2/FB-2, PA-2/PB-2, RS-3, and RSC-3, along with two new switcher types, S-3, and S-4, which primarily differed from their S-1/S-2 counterparts through the use of a new truck style. On the urging of the American Association of Railroads, Alco discontinued its Blunt truck and adopted a standard cast-steel truck designed

In 1961, a year after the Erie-Lackawanna merger, an Alco PA in full Erie paint idles at Lackawanna's Hoboken Terminal on the Jersey side of the Hudson opposite Manhattan Island. On the left is a set of Lackawanna F3s, and looming through the smog is the famous Empire State Building. The Erie and Lackawanna railroads actually consolidated their passenger facilities prior to their merger. *Richard Jay Solomon*

by General Steel Casting that was used by most other builders for switchers. This truck featured a rigid bolster and dropside equalizer, and is often described as an AAR truck.

The FA-2 carbody was two feet longer than the FA-1, providing room for passenger equipment including a boiler for steam heat. (Passenger-equipped locomotives carried an FPA-2/FPB-2 designation.) Like the later FA-1/FB-1s, these locomotives used the turbocharged 244 engine rated at 1,600 horsepower, but employed improved generators and better traction motors that permitted 52,500 pounds maximum continuous tractive effort. A four-unit FA-2/FB-2 was rated at 6,400 horsepower, significantly more powerful than EMD's comparable F7s. In 1953 Alco ceased domestic production of the FA/FB, in favor of its road-switcher designs. FPA-2/FPB-2s were produced at Montreal Locomotive Works in Canada until 1955, when they were supplanted by the 1,800-horsepower FPA-4/FPB-4 that used Alco's 251 engine (see below). Alco built more than 1,200 four-axle full-carbody freight and passenger locomotives. An impressive total, and more than twice as many as Baldwin's and F-M's combined total, yet a poor showing compared to General Motors. EMD outsold Alco more than six to one in this locomotive category alone.

The RS-3 resembled the RS-2 in most respects and shared its semi-streamlined hood design, but reflected the same variety of internal specification changes applied to the

A pair of Alco PA-1s lead a Nickel Plate Road passenger train near Cleveland, Ohio. To the left are New York Central's tracks—electrified until the mid-1950s; on the right are the electrified tracks of Cleveland Rapid Transit. *Tim Doherty collection*

In a classic scene, photographed about 1961, Erie-Lackawanna RS-3 No. 927 leads a suburban consist of Stillwell cars across a bridge in northeastern New Jersey. *Richard Jay Solomon*

Lehigh Valley served Alco's McIntosh & Seymore engine plant at Auburn, New York, and for many years was a significant Alco customer. In July 1964 a set of Lehigh Valley FA/FB cabs rolls through Whitehall, Pennsylvania. *Richard Jay Solomon*

FA-2/FB-2. The RS-3 was markedly more popular than Alco's earlier road switchers. Alco built 1,330 RS-3s between 1950 and 1956, when it introduced its more powerful RS-11. While never as common as EMD's ubiquitous "Geeps," the RS-2 and RS-3 were employed in a great variety of service all around the country. They hauled passenger trains through the Connecticut River Valley, moved coal in West Virginia, wandered prairie branchlines with locals and mixed trains, and hauled a multitude of suburban commuter trains to America's largest cities. Sounds of Alco's 244 could be heard on railroads everywhere, toiling away in place of the syncopated hiss made by an earlier generation of Alco product.

Six-Motor Locomotives

Baldwin was the first major builder to commercially introduce six-motor locomotives, starting in 1948. Alco embraced this type commercially in 1951, shortly after it discontinued its four-motor, six-axle RSC-3. EMD was the last to introduce a six-axle, six-motor model (see SD7 sidebar), but in the 1960s adopted the design on a large scale, selling thousands of six-motor locomotives. By the 1990s, six-motor units represented the vast majority of new locomotive orders,

and with the exception of passenger locomotives, the large builders had focused their domestic production on six-motor diesels. But in the early 1950s, six-motor locomotives were still viewed as a specialty item. Alco was not a stranger to the six-motor concept, and was in fact one of the first companies to build such a locomotive, producing a six-motor version of the RS-1 for the U.S. Army in World War II. Flaws with the six-axle truck design that prevented easy access to the center traction motor discouraged Alco from selling six-motor RS-1s for domestic use.

Alco entered the domestic six-motor market with the 1,600-horsepower RSD-4. Essentially it was an expanded version of the RS-3 using a 12-cylinder 244 operating at 1,000 rpm, and a tri-mount truck design that embraced a three-point suspension system. This provided a smooth ride and locomotive stability at speeds up to 60 miles per hour, while providing uniform weight distribution on all axles. The RSD-4 weighed 360,000 pounds, and therefore placed 60,000 pounds on each axle. Unlike the RSC models, the RSD-4 benefited from the full weight of the engine on its driving wheels, and developed 78,750 pounds maximum continuous tractive effort at 5.5 miles per hour, compared

In the early 1950s the full carbody or "cab unit" lost favor to the road-switcher "hood" style locomotive. Road switchers were more versatile and cost less to maintain than cab units. Chesapeake & Ohio EMD F7As and a Louisville & Nashville Alco RS-3 seen here at Covington, Kentucky, on July 27, 1958, clearly represent the difference in these two locomotive types. The F7 and RS-3 models were both built during the transition period between cabs and hoods. *Richard Jay Solomon*

Alco PA

Many observers consider the Alco PA the best-looking diesel ever built. Its impressive 6-foot snout and streamlined design was Alco's postwar entry into the long-haul passenger locomotive market—a natural evolution of its DL109 locomotive offered before the war. Its turbocharged 244 engine uttered a distinctive sound and had a propensity to bellow clouds of black smoke, making it popular with railroad enthusiasts and photographers.

The passenger diesel had been defined by Electro-Motive's E-unit, introduced in the mid-1930s. Like the E, Alco's PA (cab)/PB (booster) were carbody units, designed to operate in multiple on new streamlined trains. And, like the E-unit and other passenger locomotives of the period, the PA rode on six-axle A1A trucks; however, where the early Es required two 900-horsepower EMD 567 engines to generate 1,800 horsepower, the PA-1/PB-1s were capable of producing 2,000 horsepower with a single Alco 244 prime mover. As the horsepower race continued, Alco introduced its slightly more powerful PA-2/PB-2, which produced 2,250 horsepower with the 244 engine.

The PA/PB model designations were only applied to this famous locomotive at the very end of its production life. Alco generally referred to the locomotives with their specification numbers: PAs were DL-304, and PBs were DL-305; "A" through "D" suffixes were added to delineate model adjustments to primary components as the PA/PB design was refined.

The first PA was advertised as Alco's 75,000th locomotive, and eventually sold to Santa Fe. Except for three locomotives sold to Brazil, all of Alco's PA/PBs went to domestic lines. They were not as

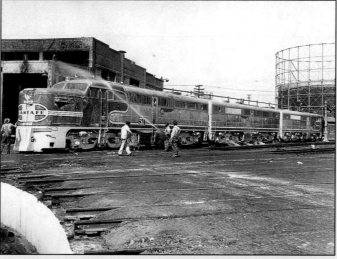

Alco's first PAs: Santa Fe's three-unit number 51, seen here in October 1946 being washed at the Redondo Junction roundhouse in Los Angeles in preparation for public display at Exposition Park. PAs served Santa Fe for more than 20 years. Fletcher Swan, Tim Doherty collection

popular as the E-units— Alco produced just 297 PA/PBs (including the three exports) compared to more than 1,200 E-units—yet the PA/PBs were used on many high-profile passenger trains. They could be found on the Erie, Gulf Mobile & Ohio, Katy, Lehigh Valley, Missouri Pacific, New Haven, New York Central System, Nickel Plate Road, Pennsylvania Railroad, Southern Railway, Southern Pacific (and subsidiary Cotton Belt), Union Pacific, and Wabash. Later Erie-Lackawanna inherited Erie's PAs, and Delaware & Hudson acquired four Santa Fe PAs. These four locomotives were the last PAs to operate in the United States, and were frequently used to haul Amtrak's *Adirondack.* They were rebuilt by Morrison-Knudsen in the late 1970s and redesignated as PA-4s before they were sent to Mexico. As this was written, there were efforts under way to repatriate and restore some of the former D&H PAs.

While intended as passenger locomotives, the PAs later found assignment as freight haulers, too. The PRR reclassified some of its PAs for freight work, often assigning them as helpers on its Elmira Branch. Union Pacific, New Haven, Erie-Lackawanna, and Nickel Plate all used PAs to haul through freights.

PA Statistics:
Builder: Alco-GE
Engine: Alco 16-cylinder 244
Horsepower: 2,000/2,250
Wheel Arrangement: A1A—A1A
Length: 65 feet, 8 inches
Total built (PA and PB): 297

Only a few weeks after the Delaware & Hudson expanded its operations to Buffalo, a quintet of D&H RS-3u's lead a westbound mixed freight (symbol AB-91) on the former Erie Railroad at Addison, New York. Morrison-Knudsen rebuilt D&H RS-3s, exchanging old 244 engines for newer 251s, and lowering the short hood, among other modifications. *Bill Dechau, Doug Eisele collection*

An Alco RS-3 and EMD GP35 are seen at Reading's hump yard at Rutherford, Pennsylvania, on September 9, 1973. Alco's RS-3 used the 244 engine. *R.R. Richardson, Doug Eisele collection*

with the RSC-3's 52,500 pounds at 8.5 miles per hour (using a 74:18 gear ratio).

In 1952 Alco upgraded its six-motor offering with the RSD-5, reflecting nominal specification changes, with similar characteristics to the RSD-4. Alco built a total of 240 RSD-4/RSD-5s between 1951 and 1956 (203 for domestic use), representing a significant portion of the six-motor diesel locomotive market at that time.

Alco was less successful with its 2,250-horsepower RSD-7, introduced as competition to F-M's powerful six-motor H24-66 Trainmaster. This locomotive was the first to feature a new semi-streamlined hood design. The hood was noticeably taller than earlier Alco road switchers. Despite its greater power, Alco's high-horsepower six-motor drew little interest, so Alco boosted RSD-7's horsepower to 2,400 in order to match the Trainmaster's output. Alco only sold 17 RSD-7s for use in North America, compared to 127 F-M Trainmasters. The market for a high-horsepower six-motor had not yet developed, but within a decade this type of locomotive would become one of the hottest sellers. Alco soon introduced improved six-motor designs using its new 251 engine, but was unable to capture a large portion of this market in the United States. As the market matured, EMD demonstrated its superiority in the six-motor locomotive category.

Alco 251 Engine

Alco developed the 251 engine in 1951 to correct flaws on the 244 engine and improve its performance. The 251 integrated the best features of the failed 241 design with the more successful 244 engine. Among the improvements were

Southern Pacific was one of only six railroads that bought Alco's six-motor RSD-15 (specification No. DL-600B), a type that suffered from relatively poor sales, with only 85 built. In later years SP relegated RSD-15s to yard work in Oregon. Here SP 3100 is seen at Eugene, Oregon, on August 19, 1975.
Brian L. Jennison

external fuel injection lines. Initially, Alco applied an inline six-cylinder 251A engine to its new switcher models. The S-5, built in 1954, was the first locomotive to receive the 251, and used it to produce 800 horsepower. The S-6, introduced a year later, was rated at 900 horsepower. While neither model sold as well as earlier switchers, the comparatively low-stress environment of a diesel switcher gave Alco the opportunity to flush out problems with the new design. In 1956 Alco introduced several new road switchers that used the 251 in place of the older 244. Alco's Canadian subsidiary, Montreal Locomotive Works, continued to use the 244 engine after Alco had switched to the 251. Furthermore, MLW built a number of models, such as the RS-10 and RS-18, that were not offered in the United States.

Alco's RS-11 supplanted the RS-3 as its basic four-axle road switcher. It employed a 12-cylinder, V-configuration 251B engine that produced 1,800 horsepower. Using a 65:18 gear ratio and 40-inch wheels, it delivered 46,500 pounds starting tractive effort at 12 miles per hour. The RS-11 used the same tall streamlined hood style introduced on the RSD-7, yet some later locomotives were delivered with a low short hood for improved visibility. This was among the first applications of a low short hood—a feature that soon became standard for road switchers on most American railroads.

Depew, Lancaster & Western superintendent Doug Eisele works the controls of DL&W RS-11 1800 in January 1999. A western New York shortline, DL&W is one of many small railroads that still prefer to use Alco locomotives.

Depew, Lancaster & Western Alco RS-11 No. 1804 clears snow on the former Lehigh Valley mainline in Batavia, New York.

Opposite
Montreal Locomotive Works was Alco's Canadian subsidiary. In October 1964 Canadian Pacific FA-2 4082 rolls west of Montreal, Quebec, near Dorval.
Richard Jay Solomon

5

BALDWIN

MATTHIAS BALDWIN BEGAN building steam locomotives in the 1830s, and for more than 120 years his name was synonymous with American locomotives. The Baldwin Locomotive Works was the foremost locomotive builder in the world during the height of the steam era. It constructed tens of thousands of locomotives for use in the United States and around the world, and its products were known for quality.

In the first two decades of the twentieth century, Baldwin shifted its production facilities from Philadelphia to the nearby suburb of Eddystone. In the 1920s, under the direction of president Samuel Vauclain, Baldwin modernized and expanded its Eddystone facility, in anticipation of brisk locomotive sales in coming years. Vauclain was a proud man, with firm convictions in the power and supremacy of the steam locomotive. In the 1920s, when the first diesel switchers entered the railroad venue, Vauclain acknowledged their potential, but felt they were no threat to steam power, and that steam would continue to play an important role in American railroading for decades to come. In the mid-1920s, Baldwin built two experimental diesels, but did not make a serious effort to enter the heavy diesel switcher market. Instead

Baldwin relied on its Whitcomb subsidiary to construct lightweight industrial switchers, typically small gasoline-mechanical locomotives, and later small diesel-electrics.

Baldwin's strong steam bias, reinforced by generations of steam men like Vauclain, made it difficult for the company to recognize the strength and potential of the diesel-electric locomotive. Baldwin remained committed to steam even after Electro-Motive demonstrated a viable diesel-electric market. Gradually Baldwin entered the diesel market, but its delay in doing so, coupled with a distrust of diesel-electric technology and steam-minded management, inhibited its ability to produce exceptional diesel-electric locomotives. According to Albert Churella, Baldwin's traditional steam-locomotive manufacturing methods were poorly suited to diesel production. Where Electro-Motive focused on just a few standardized model types, mass producing them in large numbers, Baldwin approached the diesel market as it had the steam locomotive market by working with railroads to design locomotives suited to their specific needs. Consequently, Baldwin offered the most diverse and eclectic line of diesel locomotives in the United States. It produced many different models, some with extremely small production runs.

This Pennsy DR-6-4-20 shark was photographed in the spring of 1964. Pennsylvania Railroad's unique fleet of six-axle Baldwin passenger sharks was initially assigned to the premier railroad trains west of Harrisburg. In later years they were relegated to commuter work on the New York & Long Branch between Bay Head Junction and South Amboy, New Jersey. *Richard Jay Solomon*

Baldwin's best diesels were its switchers. A pair of Baltimore & Ohio's World War II–era Baldwin VO1000s work in Philadelphia on April 20, 1958, only a few miles from the sprawling Eddystone plant where they were built. Unable to compete with EMD and Alco, Baldwin exited the diesel market in 1956. *Richard Jay Solomon*

Unfortunately for Baldwin, specialization did not result in superior performance, and in most respects Baldwin diesels were inferior to Electro-Motive and Alco products. Early on, Baldwin diesels gained a reputation for poor reliability that was not totally deserved. While some World War II–era VO model switchers suffered from poor production quality, many of its switchers performed reliably. They were ideally suited for slow-speed, heavy-service applications, and many postwar Baldwin switchers saw more than 25 years of heavy service. In 1972, *TRAINS* magazine reported there were roughly 600 Baldwin locomotives still operating, some in their third decade of service. Although the Class I carriers had retired most of their Baldwins by 1980, a number of shortline railroads continued to use Baldwin power into the mid-1990s, approximately 40 years after Baldwin had ceased diesel-electric production.

Early Baldwin Diesels

In 1931, Baldwin acquired diesel-engine builder I. P. Morris & De La Vergne for its diesel-engine design. The De La Vergne VO-series four-cycle diesel-engine was adapted for diesel locomotive applications. In 1936, Westinghouse agreed to be Baldwin's primary electrical supplier, and discontinued its own line of diesels using the Scottish Beardmore diesel engine (see Chapter 2). Initially Baldwin experienced operational difficulties with the 12.75x15.5-inch VO engine and built few commercial diesels until 1939 when it introduced two diesel switchers models. Its VO660 locomotive was 45 feet long and employed a six-cylinder VO engine that produced 660 horsepower and developed 28,000 pounds continuous tractive effort at 6.5 miles per hour. The

VO1000 was similar, though 3 feet longer. It used an eight-cylinder VO engine to produce 1,000 horsepower and develop 33,600 pounds tractive effort at 8.3 miles per hour. Both engines operated at a maximum 600 rpm.

Before World War II, Baldwin had begun drawing up plans for road locomotives and a more powerful diesel engine, but had not progressed far when the War Production Board limited the company's wartime diesel locomotive production to the two switcher types. During the war, Baldwin's efforts were focused on production rather than development, and in addition to an array of military machinery for the war effort, the company built 397 diesels and roughly 1,200 steam locomotives. However, it did develop some new engines and road diesel prototypes in preparation for the postwar market.

The 600-series Engine

In late 1945 Baldwin introduced its 600-series engines designed to power the majority of its postwar locomotives. This new engine allowed Baldwin to compete more effectively in the road locomotive market. It used the same basic parameters as the VO but was significantly more reliable, and with a turbo-supercharger, demonstrably more powerful. Initially, three models were built: 606NA, a six-cylinder, naturally aspirated engine producing 660 horsepower; 608NA, an eight-cylinder, naturally aspirated engine producing 1,000 horsepower; and the 608SC, an eight-cylinder supercharged engine producing 1,500 horsepower with an Elliot BF44 turbocharger. A few years later Baldwin introduced the 606SC, a six-cylinder supercharged engine that produced 1,000 horsepower, designed to supersede the 1,000-horsepower 608NA. At the end of 1949, Baldwin introduced three new improved 600 series engines in conjunction with its Standard locomotive line.

Postwar Changes

After the WPB lifted restrictions on locomotive production, Baldwin introduced a variety of road locomotives to compete with EMD and Alco, entering a period of development and production that is probably the most interesting of its short diesel career. At the same time Baldwin underwent several significant corporate changes that affected its locomotive production.

Westinghouse took control of Baldwin in 1948, resulting in a new management philosophy. Baldwin and Westinghouse had a long-standing relationship dating back more than 50 years; however, Westinghouse managers viewed the diesel business differently than Baldwin's previous management did. Westinghouse discontinued a new engine design Baldwin engineers hoped would make the company more competitive; it also diversified Baldwin's product line beyond locomotives, resulting in a merger with Lima-Hamilton in 1950. Baldwin's primary interest was not the acquisition of

Lima-Hamilton, successor to the Lima Locomotive Works that built many of the nation's finest modern steam locomotives, entered the heavy diesel-electric market in 1949. The company merged with Baldwin in 1950 and ceased locomotive production in 1951 after building just 174 diesel-electrics. Erie 659 is a 1,000-horsepower switcher built in 1949. Steve Gary, *J.R. Quinn collection*

The Sierra Railroad, a California shortline operating in the bucolic rolling foothills of its namesake mountains, was among the last operators of Baldwin switchers in the United States. On April 2, 1993, a Sierra S-12 leads a train of empty wood-chip cars upgrade east of Hetch Hetchy Junction. The S-12 was Baldwin's 1,200-horsepower switcher built from 1951 to 1956.

Lima's diesel locomotive business, which represented a very small segment of the locomotive market and duplicated Baldwin's own efforts, but rather L-H's other heavy machinery product lines. Following the merger, Lima's locomotive facility ceased production although locomotives built after the merger carried Baldwin-Lima-Hamilton builder's plates, the name of the newly merged company.

Baldwin's Colorful Catalog

Between 1945 and 1950 Baldwin used a numerically complex but descriptive model designation scheme to identify its locomotives. Not all of the designations used today to identify Baldwin locomotives were necessarily applied by the builder at the time of construction. Furthermore, there are some small inconsistencies in the literature on Baldwin model designations. The basic system uses a letter prefix that describes the locomotive's intended service, followed by a sequence of three numbers separated by dashes indicating the number of axles, traction motors, and horsepower. Typical prefixes are DS for diesel switcher, DR for diesel road, DT for diesel transfer, and so on. Therefore a DRS-6-4-1500 is a diesel road switcher with six axles, and four motors, delivering 1,500 horsepower. Some sources use just a two-digit horsepower indication—20 for 2,000 horsepower, for example. If a locomotive had more than one engine, the engine horsepower was followed by a slash and the number of engines, such as 1000/2.

Baldwin introduced its new Standard line in 1950, and simplified its designation system by implementing new prefixes and shorter designations. The "D" for diesel was dropped, reflecting Baldwin's exit from the domestic steam locomotive market in 1949, and standard prefixes became RS for road switcher, RF for road freight, AS for all service, and RT for road transfer. The letter suffix was followed by a two- or three-digit number indicating axles and horsepower. Locomotives were assumed to have four axles and four motors unless otherwise specified. An AS-16 was a 1,600 horsepower, four-axle, four-motor all-service road switcher, while an AS416 was a similar locomotive fitted with A1A-A1A trucks (four motors, six axles), and an AS-616 had six motors and an equal number of axles.

The Standard line included a variety of specification changes, model upgrades, and the introduction of a new 600 series engine design. This move was coincident with similar model upgrades implemented by other builders.

Switchers and Road Switchers

The 600-series engine was employed in all types of Baldwin locomotives. Baldwin's postwar switcher line consisted of the DS-4-4-660 and DS-4-4-1000, replacing the earlier VO switchers. In 1950 Baldwin boosted the output with the introduction of its S-8 and S-12 switcher (delivering 800 horsepower and 1,200 horsepower, respectively).

Baldwin also offered a complete line of B-B, A1A-A1A, and C-C road switchers with horsepower ratings from 1,000 to 1,500 in the 1945 to 1950 period, and as high as 1,600 horsepower after 1950. Among its best-selling road switchers was the six-motor 1,600-horsepower AS616, built between 1950 and 1955; 148 were sold domestically. Baldwin was the first American builder to offer a commercial six-motor road locomotive, several years ahead of its competition. This was one of the few model types with which Baldwin set an industry trend.

Baldwin was an early pioneer in the road switcher market, but its road switchers could not compete with EMD and Alco. Shortly after EMD introduced its enormously successful GP9 and SD9, Baldwin exited the locomotive market.

Transfer Locomotives

The transfer locomotive was an early specialty model designed for slow-speed, high-tractive applications such as movements between yards. The type warranted some interest into the early 1950s. (EMD addressed this application with "cow-calf" semi-permanently coupled switcher and booster combinations.) Baldwin's early efforts with six-axle, six-motor diesels were ideally suited to the transfer concept. In the mid-1940s, it developed a bidirectional dual-engine high-hood center cab transfer locomotive for the Elgin, Joliet & Eastern—a Chicago area belt line that served steel mills and transferred freight between yards. EJ&E wanted to replace steam locomotives in drag service, hauling very heavy freight trains at slow speed.

The first Baldwin DT-6-6-1000/2 (variously listed as DT-6-6-20 and DT-6-6-2000) was built in 1946 using a pair of 1,000-horsepower 608NA engines, while subsequent models employed a pair of supercharged 606SC engines to achieve the same output. Production DT-6-6-1000/2s were 74 feet long and weighed between 354,000 and 375,000 pounds, depending on the ballast option requested by the railroad. They typically delivered 64,000 pounds maximum continuous tractive effort at 9.4 miles per hour. In 1950, the DT-6-6-1000/2 was succeeded by the 2,400-horsepower RT-624, which had a similar appearance but employed 1,200-horsepower 606A engines. The Pennsylvania Railroad operated the largest fleet of transfer locomotives, including 24 Lima-Hamilton units rated at 2,500 horsepower. They were primarily used in mineral service around Mingo Junction, Ohio, and in western Pennsylvania.

Passenger Locomotives

To compete with EMD Es and Alco's PA/PB, Baldwin introduced its own 2,000-horsepower A1A-A1A passenger locomotive designated DR-6-4-20 (or DR-6-4-2000). While it sold very few, the DR-6-4-20 was built in several distinctive styles. Central Railroad of New Jersey had six double-ended "baby face" cab DR-6-4-20s, designed for suburban commuter service. Although this style was very popular

Opposite
On the morning of July 28, 1958, a pair of Chesapeake & Ohio's Baldwin AS-616 six-motor road switchers lead a coal drag through Covington, Kentucky. Baldwin was the first builder to market six-motor locomotives domestically. Baldwin's AS-616s developed 78,750 pounds continuous tractive effort at 6 miles per hour, making them ideally suited for slow-speed heavy drag work.
Richard Jay Solomon

Unique to American railroading were Central Railroad of New Jersey's six double-ended "babyface" cab DR-6-4-20s used in commuter service. While double-ended cab units are common in many countries, the style was never popular for diesels on American lines. *J.R. Quinn collection*

Raymond Loewy to resemble the railroad's streamlined T1 Duplex steam locomotives. These engines were the first of several models to receive the classic "Sharknose" design, an example of Baldwin's interest in working with customers' unique demands rather than producing more cost-effective standardized designs. While fewer than 40 DR-6-4-20s were built, no two customers received locomotives with exactly the same specifications. Among the variations were at least four different carbody styles and three different engine types. (During this same construction period, EMD built 428 E7As that were virtually identical in every respect, except for certain minor customer preferences such as headlight and pilot configurations, and of course paint scheme.) Baldwin also built a small number of 1,500-horsepower A1A-A1A "baby face" cab units for New York Central and Seaboard. These locomotives were notoriously unsuccessful and gained the uncomplimentary moniker of "Gravel Gerties" on the New York Central, presumably describing their rough riding characteristics.

elsewhere in the world, these unique locomotives were the only double-ended streamlined, full carbody diesel locomotives ever built for operation in North America. (Double-ending was typical for straight electrics, however.) Pennsylvania ordered a small fleet of DR-6-4-20s styled by

Centipedes

The most unusual diesel-electric locomotive to ever roll on American rails was Baldwin's unorthodox DR-12-8-1500/2 (sometimes designated DR-12-8-3000), a locomotive

Raymond Loewy's Sharknose was first used on Pennsylvania Railroad's T1 duplex steam locomotive. The PRR had the largest fleet of Baldwin Sharknose diesels. On July 11, 1958, crews service a set of DR-4-4-15s at Kinsman Yard in Cleveland, Ohio. *Richard Jay Solomon*

universally known as a "Centipede." It used a 2-D+D-2 wheel arrangement, and featured an articulated frame for its eight powered axles. The design stemmed from a World War II attempt at building a single-unit 6,000-horsepower high-speed passenger locomotive capable of attaining a top speed of 117 miles per hour. Originally the locomotive was to employ eight V-8 engines and generators in modular design. By 1943, Baldwin had given up on this unusual configuration, but aspects of the design were revived when the Seaboard Air Line expressed interest in the multiple-axle locomotive. So Baldwin developed a two-engine, 3,000-horsepower, 12-axle, baby face behemoth measuring 91 feet long, weighing nearly 600,000 pounds.

Seaboard bought 14 Centipedes, which it primarily used in freight service. National Railways of Mexico (NdeM) and Pennsylvania Railroad also bought Centipedes, initially for passenger service and later assigning them to heavy freight duties. The PRR dressed the locomotives in its Brunswick Green and Loewy stripes, similar to its GG1 electrics. They used a 22:57 gear ratio for 100 miles per hour operation and worked name passenger trains west of Harrisburg to Chicago and St. Louis. However, they were ill suited to this work and after a few years were regeared with a 15:63 arrangement and assigned to freight work. Toward the end of their careers, most Centipedes were being used by PRR as helpers over its famous Horseshoe Curve between Altoona and Johnstown, Pennsylvania. PRR retired its Centipedes in 1962, while NdeM's operated those in its fleet until the early 1970s. Baldwin had hoped its Centipedes would have wider appeal and Union Pacific actually ordered two but canceled the order prior to delivery. Baldwin briefly used these last two as demonstrators but failed to generate additional interest.

In later years, Pennsylvania Railroad assigned two pairs of Baldwin Centipedes to ore train service between Philadelphia and Paoli, Pennsylvania. *Richard Jay Solomon*

A pair of Central Railroad
of New Jersey Baldwin baby face
DR-4-4-15 cabs lead a freight at an
unspecified location. CNJ owned 15
of the 105 DR-4-4-15s built. Only
CNJ and Missouri Pacific operated
this model with the baby-face
carbody; the later DR-4-4-15s were
built using the Sharknose design
(see photo below). *John Krause,
Tim Doherty collection*

Baldwin DR-4-4-15 "Sharknose"
demonstrators—other than the
Loewy-styled carbody, these
locomotives were essentially the
same as baby face DR-4-4-15s. The
four Baldwin demos were eventually
sold to Elgin, Joliet & Eastern, which
subsequently sold them to Baltimore
& Ohio. *J.R. Quinn collection*

Road Freight Cabs

Baldwin had better luck with four-axle road freight cabs designed to compete with EMD's F-units and Alco's FAs, than it did with either its A1A-A1A locomotives or Centipedes, although sales were still poor compared to its competition.

Its initial offering was the DR-4-4-1500, a 1,500-horsepower locomotive built in both "A" and "B" unit configurations, powered by a supercharged 608SC engine working at 625 rpm. They measured 53 feet, 6 inches long, weighed 250,000 pounds (less than half the weight of a Centipede), and, using a 15:63 gear ratio, produced 42,800 pounds of continuous tractive effort at 10.5 miles per hour. Early DR-4-4-1500s used a baby-faced carbody configuration that resembled EMD's F-unit (at first glance one might mistake this Baldwin product for its more successful competition). Later, Baldwin applied the Sharknose carbody similar to its DR-6-4-20s built for PRR. In 1950, Baldwin's 1,600-horsepower RF-16 superseded the DR-4-4-1500 using the Sharknose carbody. Between 1947 and 1953, Baldwin sold 265 four-axle road freight cabs for domestic use.

Late Era Experiments

Baldwin ceased production of diesel-electric locomotives in 1955, ironically the same year it stopped building steam locomotives for export. In 1956 and 1957 Baldwin attempted to market a diesel-hydraulic design, and it built three lightweight power cars for New York Central and New Haven passenger trains. These used V12 Maybach engines and Mechydro hydraulic transmissions, both from Germany.

At this time, lightweight passenger trains were being promoted as a way to resuscitate American passenger services. The concept had worked well in the 1930s with the *Streamliner* and *Zephyr*, but failed miserably in the 1950s. The failure of these experiments, and lack of interest in Baldwin's imported diesel-hydraulic technology, finally ended Baldwin's long locomotive building career.

In 1956 New York Central promoted its new lightweight trains on the cover of its system passenger schedules. On the left is GM's Aerotrain, on the right is the Xplorer, powered by a Baldwin diesel hydraulic. *Richard Jay Solomon collection*

Delaware & Hudson acquired a pair of ex-New York Central Baldwin RF16 from the Monongahela in 1974, and operated them in regular freight service until selling them in 1978. Both D&H Sharks are seen on the Lehigh Valley at Tioga Center, New York, on October 3, 1975. The semaphore and tracks in the foreground belonged to Erie-Lackawanna. *Bill Dechau, Doug Eisele collection*

6

FAIRBANKS-MORSE

FAIRBANKS-MORSE'S SHORT, unprofitable career building diesel locomotives might just have been a footnote in the diesel story if it were not for the unusual prime mover it employed, and the highly advanced product it sold, albeit too early for the market's demands. Like the other diesel locomotive builders, Fairbanks-Morse (F-M) was a familiar name in railroading long before it had anything to do with diesel locomotives. The company's roots dated back to the 1830s, and it originally produced scales. Later the company was involved in the building and marketing of a variety of mechanical equipment. By 1893, F-M was selling gasoline engines for railcars. Among F-M's wide array of railroad supplies were its track equipment, including work cars, velocipedes, and handcars with the familiar walking beam power lever. The last device—long a favorite of cartoonists and movie makers—no doubt achieved far wider recognition than any of its diesel-electrics. F-M later built gasoline engine-powered railcars and small industrial gasoline-mechanical locomotives.

In 1922 F-M entered the diesel engine market, building engines for stationary and marine applications. In the 1930s, it developed a two-cycle opposed piston engine ideally suited for Navy submarines. In an opposed piston engine, each cylinder contains two pistons that face one another, with no cylinder heads. The design has several potential advantages over more conventional diesel engine designs. It requires fewer moving parts, enjoys superior heat dissipation, operates at a lower piston speed, and involves a simpler overall design.

In the late 1930s, F-M was involved with two diesel engine railroad projects. It provided opposed-piston engines for six railway motor cars built for the Southern Railway by the St. Louis Car Company. It also provided a more conventional diesel engine for a single diesel-electric center cab switcher built by St. Louis Car for the Reading. Westinghouse electrical gear was employed in both projects. Neither was particularly successful because of poor sales and the advent of World War II.

By 1940, F-M was the second largest diesel engine builder in the United States, and during World War II the company provided a large number of engines for submarines and other military applications. To accommodate its booming production, F-M greatly expanded its capacity, particularly at its Beloit, Wisconsin, factory. By 1943, F-M recognized that it would need to find civilian applications for its

Pittsburgh & West Virginia H16-44 91 pauses on the turntable at Rook, near Pittsburgh, Pennsylvania. This locomotive, built in 1956, was not yet two years old when this photo was taken on July 6, 1958. The popularity of the road switcher rendered turning facilities largely unnecessary and many were abandoned following complete dieselization. The Pittsburgh & West Virginia was to be a link in George Gould's transcontinental rail system. *Richard Jay Solomon*

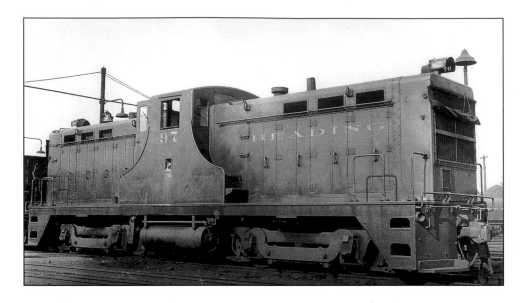

This unique Reading center-cab switcher was the first locomotive powered by a Fairbanks-Morse engine—a conventional eight-cylinder four-cycle diesel. It was built by the St. Louis Car Company in 1939, and traded back to F-M in 1953. *J.R. Quinn collection*

Although Fairbanks-Morse initially was limited to switchers, after the war F-M geared up for full production and developed a whole line of locomotives. Its postwar designs used variations of its successful 38D8-1/8 opposed-piston engine, which was being made for railroad applications in 6-, 8-, 10-, and 12-cylinder varieties. Westinghouse was F-M's primary electrical supplier until 1953-1954, when it stopped supplying electrical gear, and F-M turned to General Electric. To serve the Canadian market, F-M licensed its locomotive designs to the Canadian Locomotive Company of Kingston, Ontario. In addition to many standard F-M models, CLC also built some models solely for Canadian railroads.

"Hoods"

Fairbanks-Morse locomotive designations did not distinguish between switchers and road switchers and simply described the carbody style as a hood locomotive, a descriptive term for the carbody style (as opposed to a full carbody, or "cab" locomotive). F-M's first locomotives were H10-44 switchers. (H for hood, 10 for 1,000 horsepower, 44 for four axles and four motors. All F-M switchers and road switchers used this basic designation system.) The H10-44 was essentially patterned after Baldwin's fairly successful VO1000 switcher. Both locomotives used virtually identical mechanical specifications. The H10-44 carbody was styled by Raymond Loewy, weighed 240,000 pounds, used F-M's six-cylinder, 38D8-1/2 O-P engine with a 68:14 gear ratio, delivered

opposed-piston engines if it were to maintain its brisk engine sales. Electro-Motive's enormous success with its diesel-electric locomotives, and the enormous potential postwar market for locomotive sales, prompted F-M to ask the War Production Board for permission to construct a diesel-switcher prototype. Its request was approved, and by mid-1944 F-M had entered the heavy locomotive business.

At 10 a.m. on July 24, 1958, Southern Railway H16-44 No. 2 148 leads a short local freight through Centralia, Illinois. Southern owned just ten H16-44s. *Richard Jay Solomon*

34,000 pounds maximum continuous tractive effort at 9 miles per hour, and operated at a safe maximum speed of 60 miles per hour. The H10-44 switcher was among the F-M's most successful models. It sold 195 between 1944 and 1950, when to remain competitive, it upgraded its line and boosted output with the 1,200-horsepower H12-44.

After the war, F-M brought out a full line of four-axle, four-motor road switchers, ranging from 1,200 to 2,000 horsepower. The Canadian Locomotive Company also offered F-M road-switcher designs with A1A trucks for service on lightweight lines where low axle loadings were required. Beginning in 1947 F-M offered an unusually powerful end-cab switcher designated H20-44. Using a 10-cylinder opposed-piston engine, rated at 2,000 horsepower, F-M's H20-44 was more powerful than any other single-unit switch engine on the market. It was only nominally heavier than the H10-44, weighing in at 250,000 pounds. It could deliver 42,800 pounds maximum continuous tractive effort at 14.7 miles per hour. It looked like a switcher, but sold as a road switcher, and some lines, such as the Pittsburgh & West Virginia, operated pairs of the powerful units as road locomotives. F-M built 96 such locomotives for domestic use. F-M's midrange H15-44, a 1,500-horsepower road switcher, did not enjoy brisk sales, but in 1950 when F-M boosted the horsepower rating to 1,600 to match that of Alco's and Baldwin's new models, it became one of F-M's most

popular models, selling nearly 300 for North American service. In 1951, F-M introduced the H16-66, its first six-axle, six-motor road switcher. Perhaps F-M's best-remembered locomotive was its extremely powerful, H24-66 Trainmaster (see sidebar)—remarkable for its power, but a decade ahead of the locomotive market.

Erie Builts and C-Liners

After World War II, while F-M had enormous engine-building facilities, it only had limited locomotive erection capacity. It had sufficient space to build its switchers, but needed to enlarge its Beloit, Wisconsin, plant to accommodate additional production. As a result F-M's early road locomotives—Loewy-styled, full carbody cabs and boosters riding on A1A trucks—were assembled by General Electric under contract at its Erie, Pennsylvania, plant and were known as "Erie Builts." They were offered with four different gear ratios, and could be built for either freight or passenger service. One passenger gearing allowed for a top speed of 107 miles per hour. All were powered by a 10-cylinder O-P engine and rated at 2,000 horsepower, making them comparable to the EMD E7 and Alco's PA. The Erie Built was discontinued by 1949, when F-M's expanded Beloit plant was ready to begin production.

F-M simultaneously introduced its Consolidated Line of road locomotives, which offered a variety of customer preferences, including engine size, gear ratio, and wheel arrangement. Known as "C liners," these locomotives shared a family resemblance with the Erie Builts, but featured a foreshortened, rounded Loewy nose, and cleaner carbody styling. C-liners could be built to either freight or passenger specifications, and used 8-, 10-, or 12-cylinder O-P engines, delivering 1,600 horsepower, 2,000 horsepower, and 2,400 horsepower, respectively. Six different gear ratios were offered; using a 57:22 gear ratio, the locomotive could reach a maximum speed of 110 miles per hour. F-M's C-liner designation scheme reflected the locomotive's intended service cab or booster, horsepower, and wheel arrangement. C-liner used either a B-B arrangement or an unusual B-A1A arrangement to reduce the rear truck axle loadings when equipped with a heavy passenger steam boiler. A CFA-16-4 was a freight cab that delivered 1,600 horsepower, with four axles, while a CPA-24-5

was a passenger cab that delivered 2,400 horsepower, with four motors, but five axles.

Unfortunately for F-M, it introduced the C-liner about the time many railroads were moving away from full carbody road locomotives and specialized service. So despite its numerous customer options, the C-liner was poorly received by the industry. The C-liner was discontinued in 1953 with the introduction of F-M's powerful, versatile Trainmaster.

In 1957 and 1958, F-M built four streamlined passenger cabs, powered with its eight-cylinder O-P engine, for lightweight trains for New Haven and Boston & Maine. These were among the first passenger locomotives in North America equipped for headend power, whereby heating and electrical functions were delivered from the locomotive instead of via conventional steam lines. By the mid-1980s, headend power would become a passenger train standard.

Milwaukee Road served Fairbanks-Morse's Beloit, Wisconsin, plant and was one of F-M's best customers. On July 17, 1958, a Milwaukee Road "Erie-built" F-M cab riding on A1A trucks rests between runs at Western Avenue Yard in Chicago. Milwaukee ordered 15 of these locomotives for service on its Olympian Hiawatha. They were originally adorned with an attractive stainless-steel styling on the front. *Richard Jay Solomon*

Fairbanks-Morse Trainmaster

In 1953, Fairbanks-Morse introduced its final entry in the locomotive market: the Trainmaster, a powerful six-axle, six-motor road switcher designed to handle any mainline task on the railroad. F-M was sure it had a winner and built several demonstrators that toured around the country. These engines wore a flashy red, yellow, and black paint scheme that commanded attention. The Trainmaster, model designation H24-66, certainly had impressive characteristics. It was 66 feet long, weighed 375,000 pounds, and used F-M's powerful 12-cylinder opposed-piston engine—24 pistons, operating at 850 rpm and delivering 2,400 horsepower, the most of any single-engine road switcher on the market. Initially, it was available with three gear ratios: using a 68:15 arrangement it could deliver 78,750 pounds continuous tractive effort, and was capable of producing an astounding 112,500 pounds starting tractive effort. It rode on trimount trucks similar to those used by Alco, which distributed weight evenly using a three-point suspension system. The first Trainmasters used Westinghouse electrical equipment, but during the production run Westinghouse stopped building locomotive electrical equipment, so later locomotives used General Electric gear instead.

A pair of Norfolk & Western F-M H24-66 Trainmasters lead a passenger excursion on the former Virginian at North Clark's Gap, Virginia, on November 3, 1973. Norfolk & Western inherited F-M H24-66s from both the Virginian and Wabash, which it merged with in 1959 and 1964, respectively. N&W discontinued Virginian's electric operations in 1962. Matthew J. Herson, Jr., Doug Eisele collection

The trend toward road switchers and higher horsepower locomotives made the Trainmaster a prime candidate for the standard locomotive on many lines, but it was not to be. The railroads were not ready for a 2,400-horsepower locomotive in 1953, and the F-M locomotives were considered peculiar when compared to EMD and Alco products. Several railroads bought the H24-66, but the largest fleet (bought new) was owned by the Virginian, an Appalachian coal hauler that had a long history of buying powerful locomotives, which bought 25 Trainmasters for coal service. F-M built only 127 Trainmasters for use in the United States and Canada.

H24-66 Trainmaster Statistics:
Builder: Fairbanks-Morse
Engine: 12-cylinder 38D8 1/8 (opposed-piston)
Horsepower: 2,400
Wheel Arrangement: C-C
Length: 66 feet
Total built: 127

Fairbanks-Morse Exits the Locomotive Market

Fairbanks-Morse had hoped to capitalize on the dieselization of American railroads using its opposed-piston engine design, which had been successful in other applications. While the company was able to sell 1,256 diesel-electric locomotives, it was the least successful of the four large diesel locomotive builders in the postwar period. It consistently held fourth place in market share until 1953, when it surpassed Baldwin. At that time it had just 6.8 percent of the market, while Electro-Motive had the majority of the market, more than twice the other three builders combined. Although F-M built locomotives until 1963, it did the vast majority of its locomotive business during its first decade as a builder. It sold very few locomotives after 1957, essentially ending regular production just after Baldwin. As a whole, F-M lost money on its locomotive venture. Lukewarm sales figures never recovered the resources invested in research and development.

F-M suffered from a variety of problems. Its locomotives were plagued with a series of mechanical and engineering flaws, mostly stemming from the opposed-piston design. While this engine had proved its merit in marine applications, it was poorly adapted to the constant pounding and rigors of a railroad locomotive environment. F-M entered

Long Island Rail Road C-Liner 2006 basks in the glow of the afternoon sun on November 6, 1960, at Montauk Point, New York. Fairbanks-Morse CPA20-5 used an unusual B-A1A wheel arrangement to provide lower axle loadings for a steam boiler at the rear of the locomotive. *Richard Jay Solomon*

A pair of New Haven CPA24-5s, featuring a B-A1A wheel arrangement, depart Boston's South Station on October 5, 1951. *Bob's Photo*

The C-liner had all but vanished from North American rails by September 1971 when this photo was made—just six on the Canadian Pacific remained. A Canadian Locomotive Company–built CPA 16-4, plus a pair of H16-44s and an F-unit, lead a wood-chip "extra" near Grand Forks, British Columbia. *Mel Patrick*

the locomotive market relatively late, and was not ready for large-scale production during one of the most lucrative periods of locomotive sales. As a result, it only captured a small market share and its locomotives were generally regarded as oddballs by maintenance staffs, which exacerbated F-M's poor reliability record. However, John Kirkland in *The Diesel Builders Vol. I* suggests that F-M locomotives performed well when they were attended to by properly trained mechanics. He cites excellent F-M performance on Southern Pacific's Peninsula Line, where a fleet of Trainmasters performed reliably for two decades in extremely demanding service. Although F-Ms may have been capable of performing well given proper treatment, most roads were unwilling to invest in locomotives with special maintenance considerations, and tended to purchase from EMD and Alco. F-Ms were never common, and by the early 1970s, they were a true curiosity. Except for the odd industrial or short-line switcher, they were gone before 1980.

In 1950 Fairbanks-Morse built two P12-42 streamlined passenger cabs to power Boston & Maine's *Talgo* train. The *Talgo* employs a tilting mechanism to provide an easier ride around curves and allow higher speeds. *Richard Jay Solomon*

7

THE POWER RACE

IN LESS THAN 15 YEARS following the end of World War II, America's railroads had successfully converted from steam to diesel power. This happened much faster than many people in the industry had predicted. In the early 1950s, it was assumed that total dieselization was still more than a dozen years away. However by 1957 most lines were exclusively diesel powered, although there were a few steam strongholds that survived until 1960. Dieselization had fulfilled many of its promises, but railroads were still demanding greater efficiency.

One of the most dramatic effects of dieselization was in freight operations, where railroads made virtually all of their profits. Diesels permitted the operation of much longer trains than had been possible during the steam era. Initially railroads just sought to match the power output of steam, but soon they were exceeding steam potential by simply lashing more diesels together. The advantages of dynamic braking permitted significantly longer trains in mountainous districts. Traditional steam-era trains rarely ran more than 3,500 tons, and frequently less than that, but with diesels train weights more than doubled in a short period of time. While the FT had been intended to run in four-unit, 5,400-horsepower

sets, by the late 1950s some lines were routinely lashing together as many as a dozen F-units and GPs to move trains. Santa Fe ritually employed armies of its "covered wagons" to move trains over the California Tehachapis, and Chicago Great Western was notorious for tremendous consists of Fs rolling across cornfields in Iowa and northern Illinois.

UP GAS-TURBINES

Steam had not yet left the rails when some lines were already demanding more power than most available diesels could produce. Union Pacific, known for its insatiable appetite for power, turned to the gas-turbine for greater output. It began testing a bidirectional Alco-GE prototype in the late 1940s, and initially ordered a fleet of ten 4,500-horsepower turbines in 1950. More turbine locomotives followed from GE in 1958, rated at 8,500 horsepower, and advertised as the most powerful locomotives in the world—more powerful than any single-unit diesel-electric sold today! These gargantuan locomotives were primarily assigned to Union Pacific's busy mountain mainline between Cheyenne, Wyoming, and Ogden, Utah. While not as steep or as undulating as other mountain crossings, this exceptionally busy

EMD's GP30 featured a distinctive semi-streamlined road switcher carbody, immediately identified by the bulge on the cab roof that was essentially an extension of the dynamic brake housing. Pennsylvania Railroad bought 52 GP30s in 1963, and that September a brand-new GP30 is shown leading an eastbound freight down the "Slide" east of the tunnels at Gallitzin, Pennsylvania. *Richard Jay Solomon*

route was always an operating challenge for Union Pacific, and its high altitudes were ideally suited to the gas-turbine locomotive. Union Pacific was initially very satisfied with its turbine fleet, boasting in 1955 that it was moving roughly 10 percent of its freight with them. It later became disenchanted with the turbines, however, because of their extremely high maintenance costs and limited operating territory.

The turbines' phenomenally loud roar earned the nickname "Big Blows," and their sound made them unpopular guests in residential areas. By the early 1960s, speculation that gas-turbines might supplant diesel-electrics had diminished, and by the late 1960s the American gas-turbine had rolled its last revenue mile.

BUILDING BETTER DIESELS

The locomotive manufacturers had been gradually increasing their power output, but initially encountered a cool response to higher horsepower locomotives. At first, high-end locomotives were not dramatically more powerful, and

were often accompanied by significant reliability problems. Alco's RSD models did not sell well, nor had F-M's Train-masters. This began to change in the late 1950s, when the locomotive market dwindled dramatically after the boom years of the late 1940s and early 1950s when most lines had scrambled to replace steam power. By the late 1950s, Baldwin and F-M abandoned the new locomotive market and EMD and Alco were not filling many locomotive orders either. The largest market share was in replacing World War II–era F-units worn out after 15 years of heavy service. EMD had been rebuilding Fs since the early 1950s, but now expected to replace them with new locomotives. One incentive to get railroads to trade in older Fs was newer, more powerful diesels.

In the mid-1950s, Union Pacific ordered a large number of EMD GP9s. It hoped to obtain greater power from the design by applying turbochargers to its 567 engines to boost output from 1,750 horsepower to 2,000 horsepower. These hybrids are generally known as "Omaha GP20s" because the

One of Union Pacific's 8,500 horsepower gas-turbines leads a westbound freight toward Ogden west of Echo, Utah. *Tim Doherty collection*

A freshly shopped Southern Pacific GP20 leads the Woodland Turn onto the north leg of the Davis wye in October 1989. Southern Pacific "deturbocharged" its GP20 fleet, substituting a standard Roots blower for the turbocharger in order to reduce maintenance. This was a common practice designed to extend the service life of EMD's early turbocharged models.

Santa Fe rebuilt its SD24 fleet in the mid-1970s, replacing the older 567 engine with a more modern 645E, which boosted the horsepower rating to 2,600 and extended the life of the locomotive. In 1987 Santa Fe sold a dozen of these rebuilt units (dubbed SD26s) to Guilford. Shortly after arriving from the Santa Fe, two sets of SD24s are seen at the Delaware & Hudson's SK Yard in Buffalo, New York, on January 24, 1987.

work was performed at UP's Omaha shops, not far from where McKeen had built his railcars five decades earlier. EMD took note of UP's turbocharger experiments and introduced its own turbocharged locomotives, the 2,400-horsepower SD24 in 1958 and GP20 in 1959. While Alco had been using turbocharging for nearly two decades as a method of boosting power output, EMD had relied on supercharged engines. EMD recognized that turbocharging would be the most economical way to obtain significantly greater power from its 567 engine, and it developed the turbocharged V-16 567D2.

To compete with the GP20, Alco introduced its 2,400-horsepower RS24 in late 1959, which used a 251B prime mover. Of these more powerful models the GP20 was the most popular, but sold only 260 units, a paltry figure compared to the more than 6,000 GP7s and GP9s sold. The SD24 was less popular, although Union Pacific purchased a fleet that it assigned to its Los Angeles & Salt Lake route, a remote, heavily used desert crossing with several long, steep grades that were ill suited to UP's powerful turbine fleet. Other western lines, including the Santa Fe and Burlington, also acquired SD24s. Alco was less successful and built only

Guilford Rail System, operator of the Maine Central and Boston & Maine, maintained several former Santa Fe SD26s for mainline freight service into the late 1990s. In April 1998, SD26 643 leads a westbound freight (symbol PODH-Portland, Maine, to Delaware & Hudson) at Greenfield, Massachusetts.
Michael L. Gardner

27 RS27s, and only 35 2,000-horsepower RS32s, a model introduced in 1961.

Initially, enticing railroads to trade in old diesels for new seemed to be a more difficult task than getting them to buy new diesels to replace steam. The dramatic cost savings was not obvious. Why should a line trade in F3s for new GPs? EMD advertised the GP20 as a replacement for the F3, suggesting railroads could use just three 2,000 horsepower GP20s for four of its older 1,500 horsepower F-units, and offered cost incentives for trade-ins. Some railroads were convinced, but not enough.

GENERAL ELECTRIC'S DEBUT

In 1960, General Electric formally entered the heavy road diesel market, an unanticipated move that surprised some industry leaders, who viewed GE as a supplier of locomotive components and lightweight switchers, but not as a road locomotive manufacturer. In reality there was probably no American company better suited to enter the new diesel locomotive market than GE. It had been involved in many aspects of locomotive building for more than six decades and had a solid reputation for quality. GE had participated in almost every aspect of diesel-electric development since the dawn of diesel technology. It was responsible for the first

mainline electrification schemes, developed the first commercial American gas-electric railcars, built the first American internal-combustion locomotives, and was involved in building the first commercially successful diesel-electric locomotive. Its Erie shops had built a great variety of locomotives over the years, including the first Fairbanks-Morse road locomotives. GE's own industrial switchers were known for reliability and quality, and a number had been purchased by Class I railroads for switching and local work; some are still at work today. By 1955, virtually all diesel electrical gear was based on General Electric's designs.

General Electric's first move toward entering the heavy road diesel market was its formal break with Alco in 1953. Until that time Alco's locomotives were built as a joint venture with GE, and both company names were prominently displayed on builder's plates and advertising. According to Churella, GE's interest in building road locomotives was in part a result of Alco's failures. By 1953 General Electric had become dissatisfied with Alco's efforts. Alco locomotives had developed a reputation as second-rate products and were generally viewed as inferior to EMD's. Compounding this, Alco had lost considerable market share, and by 1954 following GE's break, Alco only held 13 percent of the new locomotive market.

General Electric wasted no time in developing its own road locomotive, but did so quietly and without announcing its intentions to enter the American market. In 1954, GE built a 6,000-horsepower, four-unit full-carbody locomotive, designated XP24-1, powered by Cooper-Bessemer four-cycle diesel engines. Two units of the four were rated at 1,200 horsepower, and two at 1,800 horsepower. This locomotive, dressed in Erie paint, was tested between Hornell, New York, and Marion, Ohio, and promoted as an experimental export locomotive. Two years later GE began marketing several locomotive types for export, ranging from 400-horsepower switchers to a 1,980-horsepower road locomotive based on the XP24-1. General Electric did not rush to introduce a domestic locomotive. Instead it refined its design, carefully evaluated the domestic locomotive market, and waited until it was ready with an appropriate product before it announced it was in the locomotive business. During the 1950s, GE refined and perfected its traction motor designs, and moved traction motor production to the Erie plant as part of an effort to consolidate its production facilities. This subtle, calculated approach is what caught the industry off guard. There was virtually nothing about GE's domestic efforts in the trade press until it unveiled its prototype.

Finally in 1960, GE rolled out its Universal line with the introduction of its 2,500-horsepower U25B for domestic use (see U25B sidebar). With this locomotive GE quickly established a foothold in the heavy locomotive market. In 1963 GE added the six-motor U25C to its catalog. GE also built an eight-axle, dual-engine locomotive, designated U50, that used a B-B+B-B wheel arrangement, and later a similar locomotive with a C-C arrangement. Union Pacific was the most interested in this type of locomotive. It bought 23 U50s (and later 46 U50Cs) and SP also acquired 3 U50s.

Initially GE's sales came at the expense of its one-time partner Alco, but GE also took some business from EMD. By the late 1960s, GE represented nearly 19 percent of the American diesel market, considerably more business than Alco had held in the mid-1950s. In time, as GE improved its

A pair of Wisconsin Central SD45s leads a Chicago-bound train up the grade toward Byron, Wisconsin. During the late 1980s and into the 1990s WC accumulated a significant fleet (more than 100) of 20-cylinder 645 locomotives, and rebuilt them at its North Fond du Lac, Wisconsin, shops. The rebuilding lowered their output slightly to improve fuel efficiency and reliability.

Southern Pacific's rugged profile was ideally suited for high-horsepower, high-tractive effort locomotives. An SD40 leading an eastbound freight over Donner Pass passes rock slide fences at Cape Horn, east of Colfax, California, in April 1990.

product line, it would overtake EMD as the nation's foremost locomotive builder.

HYDRAULICS REVISITED

Baldwin's efforts to market diesel-hydraulic locomotives in the mid-1950s had not attracted much interest, but in the early 1960s, Southern Pacific, dissatisfied with domestic high horsepower diesel-electrics, turned to Krauss-Maffei, a German locomotive builder, for diesel-hydraulics. A diesel-hydraulic uses a hydraulic transmission in place of a generator and traction motors to transmit power from the diesel engine to the wheels. In 1961 Southern Pacific and Rio Grande each imported three full-carbody Krauss-Maffei locomotives, which employed two Maybach V-16 diesel engines and a Voith hydraulic transmission system. K-M rated the locomotives at 4,000 horsepower, using a different rating system than American builders; conventional American practice would rate these locomotives at just 3,450 horsepower. While Rio Grande was dissatisfied with the hydraulics, SP placed a repeat order with K-M in 1963 for an additional 15

locomotives, using a road-switcher configuration. In 1964 SP acquired Rio Grande's three K-Ms.

SP remained interested in the potential of diesel-hydraulic power and also ordered three Alco C-643Hs (sometimes designated DH-643, specification No. DH-400), which used two 251 prime-movers and the Voith transmission to generate 4,300 horsepower. SP based its diesel-hydraulics at Roseville Yard (near Sacramento, California), intending them for heavy mountain service. However, these precision machines did not perform well hauling heavy trains in the Sierras and Cascades, resulting in short mountain-climbing careers. In later years they were primarily assigned to work in California's Central Valley. SP's diesel-hydraulic experiment was effectively ended when new high-horsepower diesel-electrics were introduced in the mid-1960s. By 1970 all the hydraulics were out of service. While the diesel-hydraulic did not attain popularity in the United States, it is still a preferred form of internal combustion power on railways in both Germany and Japan, which use straight electrics for most heavily trafficked services.

Union Pacific DDA40X 6932 races along on the Los Angeles & Salt Lake Route. This enormous, eight-axle locomotive was powered by two 16-cylinder 645E3A diesels. *Mel Patrick*

Beneath the cowl of a former Santa Fe F45 is an EMD 20-cylinder 645 prime mover capable of generating 3,600 horsepower.

EMD SD40

When EMD introduced its new line of locomotives in 1965 it changed the diesel-electric locomotive market. This line used a whole array of new components that marked a departure from EMD's incremental evolutionary changes to its earlier locomotives. They featured the new 645 engine design (instead of the 567), and new traction motors (a new AC-DC electrical system that used an alternator in place of a generator). EMD promotional literature exclaimed its new line was the "biggest development since 1939," an allusion to the debut of its enormously successful FT.

Initially, one of the biggest sellers was the supercharged 3,000-horsepower SD40. This powerful, reliable locomotive was well suited to heavy North American freight applications. It was designed to haul long heavy freights in a variety of situations, and represented a logical successor to EMD's earlier six-axle, six-motor models. Railroads embraced the SD40 because its horsepower rating allowed them to replace aging F3 and F7 diesels rated at just 1,500 horsepower—two for one—and it offered greater reliability than earlier models.

In 1966 EMD delivered 387 SD40s, an enormous number for a single model in one year. By 1967, however, the slightly more powerful SD45, rated at 3,600 horsepower, had temporally outshone the SD40—outselling it more than six to one. Only 57 SD40s were built that year. Nevertheless, difficulties with the SD45 design reversed this trend, and the SD40 resumed its place as EMD's fastest-selling locomotive until 1972, when EMD introduced its much improved Dash 2 line, and the new SD40-2 replaced the older SD40. In just six years

A former Detroit Edison SD40 wearing an EMD demonstrator paint scheme leads Grand Trunk and Duluth, Winnipeg & Pacific SD40s and two Wisconsin Central SD45s, one wearing Santa Fe paint, southbound over WC's Byron Hill, south of Fond du Lac, Wisconsin, with ballast train destined for Chicago. By the mid-1990s, many remaining SD40s had been acquired by locomotive leasing companies.

EMD sold 1,285 SD40s—200 more units than its pioneering FT had sold in roughly the same span of time. This statistic is especially impressive considering each SD40 was more than twice as powerful as each FT, and in the 1960s, EMD was competing against two other diesel builders for share of the high-horsepower road diesel market. EMD captured the lion's share of that market because its products were vastly superior to those of its competitors. The SD40-2 went on to become EMD's most popular locomotive, selling 3,945 units between 1972 and 1986.

SD40s and SD40-2s were the standard road locomotives of the 1970s and 1980s. Their exemplary performance and remarkable reliability were appreciated by the railroads, while their smooth ride, quick throttle response, and solid pulling power made them popular with locomotive engineers. However, the SD40 was often dismissed by railroad enthusiasts because of its ubiquitous presence and uniform design, and because the SD40/SD40-2 effectively replaced a great variety of earlier diesels that had populated the railroad scene in the 1950s and 1960s.

SD40 Statistics:
Builder: EMD
Engine: 16-cylinder 645
Horsepower: 3,000
Wheel Arrangement: C-C
Length: 65 feet, 8 inches/65 feet, 9.5 inches
Total built: 1,285 (includes SD40A)

HIGH HOOD VS. LOW HOOD

In the late 1950s the low short hood began to get some attention. EMD and Alco both offered road-switcher models with either option. Typically, the high short hood had been used to house auxiliary equipment such as steam generators with large boilers for passenger service. As the need for such equipment diminished with the decline of passenger service, railroads began to order locomotives with low short hoods to provide increased crew visibility. By the early 1960s low short hoods had become the standard option, although some lines such as the Southern and Norfolk & Western continued to order high short-hood locomotives for two more decades.

EMD INTRODUCES A NEW LINE

By the early 1960s, EMD recognized that it had pushed the output of its 567 engine to its practical limit. The engine had been developed in the 1930s, and initially its 16-cylinder configuration produced only 1,350 horsepower. Through gradual improvements, higher rpms and modifications such as turbocharging, EMD had nearly doubled the engine's output. In 1961 EMD introduced the GP30 with a 567D3 engine rated at 2,250 horsepower to supplant its 2,000-horsepower GP20. The GP30 employed a unique looking semi-streamlined road-switcher carbody that featured a rounded cab with a distinctive bump on the

In April 1993, Santa Fe FP45 No. 97, resplendent in Warbonnet paint, leads a westbound with another cowl unit at Sand Cut—situated at the base of Southern Pacific's grade over the California Tehachapis. EMD designed the cowl FP45 at Santa Fe's request.

Alco built a single A-B-A set of C-855s for Union Pacific. As its designation suggests, this was a 5,500-horsepower locomotive riding on eight powered axles. *Union Pacific photo, Tim Doherty collection*

The Cape Breton & Central Nova Scotia—a RailTex company that operates 236 miles of the former Canadian National line, primarily between Truro and Sydney, Nova Scotia, had one of the last fleets of six-motor Alco products, mostly former CN Montreal-built M-630s. Three CB&CNS M-630s and a GP18 roll across Ottawa Bridge en route to Sydney on July 25, 1997. By 1998 most of CB&CNS' Montreal-built locomotives were out of service.

Following pages
In the early 1970s, Southern Pacific worked with EMD to design a high-horsepower locomotive that worked better in long tunnels and snow sheds, where oxygen depletion resulted in poor performance. EMD came up with the SD45T-2, which featured air intakes at running board level instead of along the roof line. In January 1991, a Cotton Belt SD45T-2 works as a helper on a coal train traversing SP's famous Tehachapi Loop. On the upper level, an SD45, SD40T-2, SD40, and another SD45 are in the lead.

roof, and used a pressurized engine compartment. By this
time the economy had improved from its late 1950s recession, and railroads were in better shape, needing greater
motive power. In just two years EMD sold nearly 950
GP30s. In 1963, EMD introduced the GP35, using a
567D3A engine rated at 2,500 horsepower to compete with
GE's U25B. This locomotive proved even more popular than
the GP30, and sold more than 1,300 units. A year later EMD
introduced a six-motor version, model SD35, selling 360 in
less than two years. It also developed a dual-engine DD35
that was essentially two GP35s in one carbody. These were
built in both cab and booster configurations. SP bought three
and Union Pacific bought 42.

The GP30, GP35, SD35, and DD35 demonstrated significant power increases over EMD's older locomotives. In
order to sustain even greater horsepower, EMD needed a new
engine, so even as these new powerful models were filling the
erection halls at La Grange, EMD's engineers were preparing
the new-generation prime mover: the 645 engine.

This new engine represented a refinement and enlargement of the 567 engine. The cylinder bore was increased by

78 cubic inches to 645—thus the new designation. This
new engine marked a distinct departure from EMD's earlier engine designs. Throughout the postwar period EMD
had retained the same basic components when it changed
models in an effort to maintain consistency in the parts
supply. Where Alco and Baldwin had gone through a variety of primary component model changes, EMD had been
extraordinarily stable. This was one of the reasons for its
locomotives' great popularity among American railroads.

In addition to the new engine, these locomotives also employed an entirely new AC-DC electrical system that used an
alternator in place of a generator, and employed silicon diodes
to rectify the alternating current to direct current for the traction motors. This development reduced the number of parts,
decreased maintenance, and perhaps most important, allowed
for significantly higher output to traction motors. General
Electric and Alco soon followed EMD's lead and implemented similar AC-DC transmission systems. This development should not be confused with the application of practical
diesel-electric AC traction locomotives, a revolutionary development that occurred in the 1990s (see Chapter 8).

EMD SD45

In the mid-1960s a new sound thundered over American rails— EMD's 645 prime mover had come of age, and the largest of these were the unprecedented V-20 configuration in the SD45. While EMD's four-unit FTs were advertised as 5,400-horsepower locomotives, EMD's three-unit E7s as 6,000 horsepower, and Baldwin's curious, multi-drivered "Centipedes" as 6,000-horsepower locomotives, these combinations consisted of either multiple units, multiple engines per unit, or both. The SD45 was a single-engine 3,600-horsepower locomotive. From the front it shared a family resemblance with other EMD road locomotives; however, distinctive "flared" radiators at the back of the locomotive distinguished the SD45 from the rest of the EMD six-motor diesels (although the angled radiator was later used on other EMD products). The use of angled radiators was a method of obtaining greater cooling area without a significant carbody redesign.

The high-horsepower SD45 was an immediate success with railroads looking for greater power, and the type was particularly popular in the West, where greater power seemed to be in perpetual demand, demonstrated by the advent of gas-turbines, turbocharged "Omaha GP20s," experiments with diesel-hydraulics, and the dubious dual-engine eight-axle monsters of the early 1960s, not to mention some of the largest steam locomotives ever built. Great Northern received the very first SD45s in May 1966, appropriately naming it "Hustle Muscle." Southern Pacific, always searching for a way to harness greater power under a single hood with reliable results, immediately embraced the SD45 and ultimately ordered the most, a total of 367, including those lettered for its Cotton Belt subsidiary. SP went on to encourage the development of the SD45T-2 variant for better performance in tunnels. Northern Pacific, Burlington (later Burlington Northern formed by the merger of GN, NP, CB&Q, and Spokane, Portland & Seattle in 1970), Santa Fe, Rio Grande, Frisco, Milwaukee Road, Chicago & North Western, and Union Pacific all owned SD45 fleets. Eastern railroads also bought SD45s, although they

In the 1980s New York, Susquehanna & Western acquired a small fleet of former Burlington Northern SD45s. On October 14, 1988, NYS&W SD45 3614 leads a Delaware & Hudson coal train through the Canisteo River Valley near Cameron Mills, New York. In 1976 the D&H was granted trackage rights over the former Erie Railroad between Binghamton and Buffalo, New York, to provide competition with Conrail.

N Y S W
3622
SD 45

New York, Susquehanna & Western operates a small fleet of former Burlington Northern SD45s.

were less common than in the West. Pennsylvania (and later Penn Central, and Conrail), Norfolk & Western, and Southern Railway operated sizable fleets. Numerous other carriers operated SD45s in smaller numbers. The SD45's popularity waned in the late 1960s when crankshaft failures on its 20-cylinder 645 raised reliability concerns. The locomotive's voracious fuel consumption did not improve its popularity, particularly during the oil shortages of the 1970s, which initiated a new round of improved, fuel-efficiency designs.

To the observer, the SD45's most impressive qualities are its raw power potential and the unforgettable sound they make when three or more are operated in tandem. All locomotives make noise, but SD45's and its 20-cylinder kindred—SDP45, FP45, F45, SD45-2, and SP's SD45T-2—produce a low base, pulsating throb that shakes the ground, permeating the environment and penetrating the very soul of anyone with presence to listen. Hearing SD45s working a train up a long mountain grade, or rolling though a narrow canyon was one of the great experiences of train watching in the last decades of the twentieth century. By the late 1990s, few SD45s remained complete with 20-cylinder 645s—some had been rebuilt with the more efficient 16-cylinder engine, and many scrapped. Yet the SD45, now more than 30 years old, still survives on some carriers such as Wisconsin Central. The 3,600-horsepower SD45 has long been surpassed, and today far more powerful, more fuel efficient, and quieter locomotives now rule the American rails.

SD45 Statistics:
Builder: EMD
Engine: 20-cylinder 645
Horsepower: 3,600
Wheel Arrangement: C-C
Length: 65 feet, 8 inches/65 feet, 9.5 inches
Total built: 1260

A pair of U25Cs lead empty coal hoppers (train symbol XB-3) south on the former New York Central Fallbrook line through Corning, New York, on March 9, 1975. The U25C was essentially a six-motor version of GE's successful U25B. *Doug Eisele*

In 1965 EMD introduced nine new models that employed its new technology. EMD had moved away from just a handful of standard models that had represented the bulk of its production in the postwar period, instead developing a more diverse line of locomotives. As it raised the horsepower threshold, EMD felt compelled to produce specialized, medium-horsepower locomotives, and locomotives designed specifically for slow speed, high tractive-effort applications. To address divergent trends in locomotive building, EMD also offered both turbocharged and supercharged models, and four-motor and six-motor arrangements. In addition, following the discontinuation of its once-popular E-unit in 1964, it offered passenger versions of its road switchers.

The turbocharged, 16-cylinder 645E3 engine was used to develop 3,000 horsepower in the four-motor GP40 and six-motor SD40 locomotives intended to supplant the 2,500-horsepower GP35 and SD35. Supercharged, 16-cylinder 645 engines rated at 2,000 horsepower powered the GP38 and SD38. The SD45 was a 3,600-horsepower monster that pushed the horsepower threshold to a new high, using a turbocharged, 20-cylinder 645E power plant (see SD45 sidebar). Two new switchers were also offered, the SW1000 and SW1500, using supercharged 8- and 12-cylinder 645s, respectively. To serve the potential passenger market, EMD introduced the steam boiler–equipped SDP40. Easily converted to freight service, it was intended to appeal to railroads uneasy about investing money strictly in passenger

locomotives, at a time when it appeared the end was near for the American passenger train.

Within a few years EMD expanded its 645 line. A turbocharged 12-cylinder 645 was introduced in the GP39 and SD39 as a fuel saver. On request of the Santa Fe, EMD built shrouded passenger FP45s, and later, freight service F45s, both using 20-cylinder 645 engines to develop 3,600 horsepower. Unlike the F-units whose full-carbody design was structurally integral to the locomotive, these 1960s-era locomotives were simply shrouded versions of their road switcher counterparts—the shroud had no structural value.

UNION PACIFIC CENTENNIALS

The largest locomotive of the era was the gargantuan DDA40X, built for Union Pacific beginning in 1969. Known as Centennials, and numbered in the 6900 series block in honor of the 100th anniversary of the completion of the transcontinental railway—a historic moment for Union Pacific and the United States—the DDA40X locomotives were the largest and most powerful single-unit diesel-electrics in the world at the time. Measuring 98 feet, 5 inches long, they were powered by 2 16-cylinder 645E engines working at 950

On May 5, 1972, a long Penn Central freight led by a GE U25B and an Alco RS-3 slugs it out on New York's Byron Hill—one of the few grades on the old New York Central "Water Level Route," located a few miles east of Batavia, New York. *Doug Eisele*

Michigan's ore-hauling Lake Superior & Ishpeming favored six-motor models discarded by larger lines, making it popular with photographers and diesel enthusiasts. In September 1985 a U25C leads two Alco RSD-15s with an empty ore train at Eagle Mills, Michigan. *George S. Pitarys*

rpm (instead of just 900 rpm on early units), generating an astounding 6,600 horsepower. UP took delivery of 47 Centennials between April 1969 and September 1971. These locomotives used a widenose cab, an antecedent to the North American Safety Cab

ALCO'S CENTURY LINE

In 1963, Alco introduced its improved "Century" line, in what proved to be its last effort to stay in the locomotive business. The Century was a marketing scheme that incorporated a variety of minor improvements with an attractive new carbody style and a new model designation system. Among other improvements the Century used a pressurized engine compartment, following a trend started with EMD's GP30, to minimize dust and grime inside the locomotive. The carbody was designed for easy removal of primary components. Alco also introduced a new electrical system using modern electronic components that facilitated better traction, and smoother acceleration through improved wheel slip control.

The new designation system used a "C" for Century, followed by a three-digit number. The first digit represented the number of powered axles, the second and third digits represented locomotive horsepower. Thus a C-628 was a six-axle, 2,800-horsepower locomotive.

The first two four-axle models, C-420 and C-424, were essentially upgraded versions of the RS-32 and RS-27, respectively. Like the RS-32, the C-420 used a 12-cylinder 251B generating 2,000 horsepower, but it was slightly longer, measuring 60 feet, 3 inches in length. The C-420 was identifiable by its slightly longer front hood. It was built exclusively for the American market between 1963 and 1968. The C-424 used a 16-cylinder 251B to generate 2,400 horsepower. It was built in both the United States and Canada.

A pair of Lehigh Valley's Alco C-628s—known as "Snow Birds"—poses with eastbound freight LV-2 on the Route 5 overpass in Geneva, New York, on October 1, 1972. Lehigh Valley was one of several railroads remaining loyal to Alco into the mid-1960s. *Doug Eisele*

GE U25B

In 1960 General Electric entered the domestic heavy locomotive market with its high-horsepower U25B. GE was no stranger to the railroad marketplace. It had been supplying railway equipment for more than seven decades, and was instrumental in early diesel development. GE had long been a producer of small industrial and switching diesels, and had been a partner with Alco in heavy diesel construction. In 1953 the two companies quietly dissolved their partnership. While GE continued to supply electrical gear to its one-time partner, it went on to develop its own locomotive line.

The U25B used a 16-cylinder Cooper-Bessemer engine. This was a powerful turbocharged four-cycle engine with a 9x10.5-inch bore and stroke, operating at 1,050 rpm and producing 2,700 horsepower, with 2,500 horsepower available for locomotive traction. In addition to its high-horsepower rating—slightly higher than any locomotive offered by either EMD or Alco at that time—one of the big selling points of the U25 was its simplified GE electrical system. Electrical components were GE's specialty, and it had a great advantage over both its competitors. GE boasted that its new electrical system used 60 percent fewer components than those on early locomotives. It also incorporated an innovative air-filter design that set a new industry standard.

The first U25 demonstrators were unveiled in 1960, and a four-unit set made a well-publicized tour of the American West in 1961. The U25 was intended for high-speed freight operations. The first U25Bs featured high short hoods, as had most early road switchers, but Southern Pacific (which had placed the first large order for U25s) requested a low short hood, based on its experience with low-nose

Two Erie-Lackawanna U25Bs lead a short freight westbound through the Canisteo River Valley at Carsons, near Hornell, New York, on October 27, 1975. Bill Dechau, Doug Eisele collection

EMD GP9s and Alco RS11s. The short hood became a standard option, and very few U25Bs were delivered with high hoods. The U25B was a popular locomotive—476 were sold to American railroads—and it successfully launched GE in the road locomotive market. Railroads all over the country bought the U25B, and its six-motor counterpart, the U25C. In just a few years, GE replaced Alco as the No. 2 American locomotive builder.

Among U25 users were Burlington, Erie-Lackawanna, Frisco, Louisville & Nashville, New Haven, New York Central, Pennsylvania, Rock Island, Santa Fe, Southern Pacific, Union Pacific, and Wabash. By the late 1970s most U25Bs had been retired. While a few were rebuilt, most were sent to scrap. One of the last railroads to regularly use U25Bs was the Maine Central, which acquired a small fleet from the defunct Rock Island. The locomotives were painted in Maine Central's flashy yellow and green and operated across the railroad, and later all over Guilford lines when that company acquired Boston & Maine and Delaware & Hudson operations. The U25B's place in history has not been overlooked, as several of the locomotives have been preserved for posterity.

U25B Statistics:
Builder: General Electric
Engine: FDL-16
Horsepower: 2,500
Wheel Arrangement: B-B
Length: 60 feet, 2 inches
Total built: 476

In 1964, to meet a request of the Erie-Lackawanna, Alco boosted the output of the C-424 by 100 horsepower, to match GE's 2,500 horsepower U25B. The new locomotive model, C-425, used a 16-cylinder 251C engine, which operated slightly faster than the 251B, to obtain the higher power output. Erie-Lackawanna was one of six railroads to purchase this model, and a total of 91 were sold, compared to 476 U25Bs, and a total of 190 Alco and MLW C-424s (53 to U.S. railroads). While not as prolific as their precursors, the C-424 and C-425 had significantly longer careers. By the mid-1980s the U25B had effectively vanished, while many Alco and MLW Centuries toiled on well into the 1990s, and a number of short lines still use four-axle Century locomotives. Alco built 16 C-430s in an attempt to rival EMD's

GP40. Ten of these locomotives were purchased by longtime Alco supporter New York Central.

In 1966 Alco introduced the C-415, billed as a utility locomotive. This center-cab switcher was built with both normal and high-profile cabs, and powered by an eight-cylinder 251E engine. The type was not well received, and only 26 were built, compared to more than 800 EMD SW1500s, which were introduced at about the same time for essentially the same type of service.

Alco's first six-motor Century was the 2,750-horsepower C-628, powered by a 16-cylinder 251C. It was introduced in 1963, and billed as the most powerful single-engine diesel-electric, a title it held for a very short time. In 1965, Alco supplemented the C-628 with a slightly more powerful C-630

Three Union Pacific GE U30Cs and a Chicago & North Western EMD six-axle lead an eastbound coal train at Hermosa, Wyoming, on August 12, 1978. *Brian L. Jennison*

National Railways of Mexico (Ferrocarriles Nacionales de Mexico) has been a large GE customer since the 1970s. On March 20, 1975, a brand-new U36C leads a freight near El Oro, Coahuila, Mexico. *Jim Marcus, Doug Eisele collection*

The MP15 was EMD's last switcher model; it was offered with either AC or DC electrical transmission—but strictly DC traction motors. A pair of former Milwaukee Road MP15 switchers roll across the Mississippi River in Minneapolis, Minnesota, on January 14, 1994. The lead locomotive still wears fading Milwaukee paint, the other is dressed in Soo Line's "candy apple" red paint. Soo Line purchased Milwaukee Road in 1985—by the mid-1990s Soo had become part of CP Rail.

that employed an AC-DC transmission system similar to that used by the new EMD 645-powered locomotives. It was rated at 3,000 horsepower, and intended to compete with the SD40. American production ceased in 1968, although a similar model, M-630, was built in Canada until 1972. Alco and MLW sold 200 of these locomotives, including export models to Mexico. While one of Alco's most successful six-motor designs, it fared poorly in comparison to EMD's SD40, which sold more than 1,200 units, and GE's U30C, which sold roughly 600 units. The C-630's weak North American sales performance reflects Alco's difficulty competing against EMD and GE, and its waning market share.

In 1967, Alco introduced its last six-motor design, the C-636, to match EMD's SD45. It remained in American production for less than a year, selling just 34 units, while a Canadian version, model M-636, was marketed by MLW until 1975, representing an additional 100 locomotives. A number of C-636s and M-636s ended up on the remote, isolated Quebec Cartier ore-hauling line in northern Quebec, where they were beautifully maintained, and used daily to haul 14,000-ton iron ore trains through the 1990s, demonstrating that with proper care and maintenance Alco's six-motor design had a valid application. MLW built a single M-640 in

1971 for Canadian Pacific. In the mid-1980s, this unique locomotive was used as a test bed for emerging AC traction motor technology, and was one of the first AC traction diesel-locomotives built in North America.

Alco made a short-lived attempt to enter the eight-motor, double-diesel market in 1963 with an A-B-A set of eight-axle C-855s that were used by Union Pacific.

General Electric's success in the American locomotive market effectively doomed Alco, and by 1968 Alco's sales had nearly evaporated. Alco had been purchased by the Worthington Corporation in 1964, a conglomerate that produced a variety of products. Having failed in the modern locomotive business, Alco exited the market in 1969, although it continued to supply parts, and its MLW affiliate purchased Alco's designs and built new locomotives into the mid-1970s. Bombardier bought the Alco designs from MLW in the mid-1970s, and continued to build locomotives until the mid-1980s.

MORE U-BOATS

Early on, General Electric's Universal Line acquire the nickname U-boats, which applied to its U25B and all the succeeding U-models. General Electric followed the higher horsepower trend and introduced its own high horsepower locomotives to compete with EMD and Alco. The U28B and U28C were introduced in 1965, but were soon superseded by the 3,000-horsepower U30B and U30C—GE's first locomotives to employ an AC-DC transmission system similar to that used by EMD and Alco. They also featured a variety of other improvements, including a modified engine design intended to reduce the consumption of lubrication oil. Through further refinement of its AC-DC transmission system and additional engine improvements permitting faster operating speed, plus a better fuel delivery system and a new fuel injector design, GE was able to introduce 3,300-horsepower models, followed by 3,600-horsepower models, along with increased fuel efficiency.

In addition to domestic production, both GM and GE build locomotives for export. Iarnród Éireann (Irish Rail) has a large fleet of GM diesels, some more than 30 years old, such as this Class 181 built in 1966. It's an EMD JL18, a four-axle, double-ender that uses an eight-cylinder 645E rated at 1,100 horsepower. Although foreign in appearance, this 5-foot, 3-inch gauge locomotive seen at Claremorris, County Mayo, sounds very familiar to American ears.

On July 5, 1975, brand-new Maine Central U18B *Independence Class* 408, the Battle of Bagaduce, sits on the turntable at Bangor, Maine. Only a handful of railroads opted to buy GE's 1,800-horsepower "Baby Boats"; Maine Central bought ten to replace aging Alco RS-2s and RS-3s, naming them for Revolutionary War figures and events. *George S. Pitarys*

Passing Grizzly, Montana, a Burlington Northern freight works toward the summit at Marias Pass on the evening of July 7, 1994. Leading is one of BN's ubiquitous SD40-2s, the most common locomotive on the railroad. Following is a cabless GE B30-7A, a 12-cylinder "booster" type only ordered by BN. Missouri Pacific ordered similar 12-cylinder 3,000-horsepower units from GE, but with cabs. In GE lexicon, the "A" indicates a 12-cylinder 7FDL engine on a locomotive that typically would use a 16-cylinder engine.

While GE's 3,000-horsepower locomotives were well received, its higher horsepower locomotives did not sell as well. It built just 137 U33Bs and 375 U33Cs, and even smaller numbers of U36s for the American market.

MIDSIZE COMEBACK

Through the 1960s, the push was on for greater and greater horsepower with a strong trend toward six-motor locomotives. Through the 1970s, however, there remained a sizable market for midrange locomotives, especially four-axle switchers and road switchers in the more traditional 1,500-horsepower to 2,300-horsepower range. While 2,400-horsepower locomotives might have been considered high horsepower in 1953, by 1973 they had fallen to just midsize.

EMD's popular GP38 and GP38-2 demonstrated a large need for supercharged 2,000-horsepower locomotives, and sold more than 2,500 in the United States alone. GE introduced its 2,300-horsepower U23B in 1968, and built 425 by 1977. EMD's traditional switcher line was still selling well into the early 1970s, when it introduced its MP15 in 1974. This locomotive type was built with either an AC-DC or

traditional DC transmission system, depending on customer preference; it sold nearly 500 units by the early 1980s. Most MP15s used a supercharged 12-cylinder 645, but some locomotives built in the 1980s and designated MP15T used a turbocharged eight-cylinder 645 instead.

In the mid-1970s EMD was looking to recycle the vast fleets of 20-year-old GP7s and GP9s that had reached retirement age by introducing the GP15-1. Railroads were encouraged to round up their old GPs and send them to EMD for remanufacturing. In return they would get a brand-new 1,500-horsepower locomotive built with a mix of new and recycled parts. This plan met with limited success. Like the MP15, the GP15 was offered in both AC-DC and straight DC versions, with some later locomotives using the 12-cylinder turbocharged engine. All told, slightly more than 350 GP15-1s were sold. Most railroads decided to hold onto their GPs and rebuild them, or sell them for scrap.

Concurrent with EMD's GP15-1, GE introduced its 1,800-horsepower U18B. The smallest of the domestic U-boats, the U18B was just 54 feet long and powered by a diminutive eight-cylinder FDL engine. They were noted for their distinctive sound, which resembled a struggling farm tractor more than a railway locomotive. The U18B was not a popular locomotive. In production for just a little more than three years, only 163 were sold in North America, including 45 to Mexico. Seaboard Coast Line and Maine Central were among the more prominent American buyers.

REBUILDING

During the 1970s, contract rebuilding had become a profitable business, and over the next two decades several companies entered the commercial locomotive rebuild business. The cost of rebuilding a locomotive was dramatically less than a new one, and this cost savings was especially appealing when dealing with lightweight switchers, small road switchers, and other types where a new locomotive was not cost-effective. Rebuilt locomotives have been favored by shortline and regional railroads that were effectively priced out of the new locomotive market during the 1960s and 1970s. In the 1950s, rebuilt locomotives represented just a small fraction of a railroad's locomotive fleet. By the mid-1980s, however, locomotive rebuilding had grown dramatically. American Association of Railroads' statistics indicate that in 1983 Class I railroads acquired 200 new locomotives and 153 rebuilt locomotives. By 1991 this trend had reversed somewhat. That year Class I carriers acquired 472 new locomotives compared to just 131 rebuilds.

Southern Pacific was one of several lines to undertake a large-scale capital rebuild program. In the 1970s it rebuilt many of its aging GP9s, SD7s, and SD9s at its Sacramento shops. Later it expanded this program and overhauled hundreds more modern locomotives, including a large portion of its SD45 fleet. Repowering older Baldwin, Fairbanks-Morse, and Alco locomotives with more modern or more reliable engines became a popular alternative to replacement. For example in the 1970s, Penn Central initiated a program to repower its large Alco RS-3 fleet with EMD 567 engines. It undertook the majority of the work at its DeWitt, New York, shops. Penn Central's successor, Conrail, continued this work. Rebuilding and repowering locomotives sometimes results in dramatic changes in appearance, and frequently involves new model designations. In some situations a locomotive rebuild involves such extensive work that the final product is best described as "remanufactured."

Engineer's control stand in a 1960s era F45.

The engineer's controls for a Burlington Northern Santa Fe SD70MAC, typical of computerized desktop controls used on modern locomotives.

CSX was created by the combination of the Chessie System and Seaboard System, each already an amalgam of other merged railroads. To the stockholders it might be just part of CSX, but to all that know this line—paint and paychecks aside—it is the Baltimore & Ohio! CSX B36-7 5879, B30-7 5568, GP40-2 6358, and SD40-2 8000 roll westbound across the Potomac River east of Paw Paw, West Virginia. This piece of railroad, known as the Magnolia Cutoff, was built shortly after the turn of the century to better compete with the Western Maryland—a line absorbed by Chessie System in the early 1970s. One of WM's abandoned bridges can be seen in the distance.

Southern Pacific's locomotive deadlines at Taylor Yard in Los Angeles on September 22, 1980, reflect the effects of a recession that prompted railroads nationwide to store less efficient locomotives. By the time the economy improved in the early 1980s, most six-motor Alco and GE "U-boats," such as those stored here, had been sent to scrap. *Brian L. Jennison*

8

MODERN POWER

BY THE 1970s, the horsepower race had effectively topped out at 3,600 horsepower. Sales figures revealed that for the time being railroads seemed more interested in 3,000-horsepower locomotives than more powerful models, with reliability and availability larger concerns than nominal power increases. Alco had exited the American market, leaving just EMD and GE to compete for new locomotive sales.

DASH-2 AND DASH-7

In 1972 EMD introduced its Dash-2 line, six years after it began regular production of its 645-powered locomotives. The Dash-2 reflected the refinement of EMD's existing line, incorporating an array of improvements aimed at increasing locomotive reliability and lowering maintenance costs. The new locomotives did not look radically different on the outside, but EMD listed some 40 improvements and component changes associated with the new line. The external changes included the new HT-C truck, designed for higher adhesion using an improved suspension system that minimized wheel slip. The truck featured center-axle struts that look similar to automobile shock absorbers. The 645 engine was upgraded with stainless-steel

piston rings and an improved bearing design. The most significant Dash-2 improvement was a totally new electrical system that employed modern, solid-state electronic modules in place of traditional relays. Electronic control permitted fine performance adjustments. While early on EMD suffered from a variety of break-in flaws, ultimately it claimed that Dash-2 improvements provided a 10 to 15 percent increase in efficiency over older models.

General Electric responded to the Dash-2 by implementing improvements to its Universal Line, but it was far less successful than EMD. GE locomotives built in the late 1960s and 1970s were notoriously less reliable than their EMD counterparts. Since one of the main issues in locomotive operation at this time was unit availability, GE was forced to improve its product line in order to remain competitive. In 1976 GE introduced its Dash-7 line, which embodied a variety of minor improvements. Concurrent with this change, largely a marketing development like the suffix on the Dash-2, was a new model designation scheme. The "U" was dropped, the axle designation letter moved to the front, and a "-7" suffix added to the end of the model designation. Thus what had been designated as a U30C was now a C30-7,

On the afternoon of August 28, 1998, one of Union Pacific's "convertible" SD90MACs leads a westbound empty coal train near Brady, Nebraska. This locomotive was delivered with an older GM 2-cycle engine, but is designed to receive a 6,000-horsepower Deutz engine when that model becomes available. The enormous air intake vents are a trademark of GM's SD80MAC and SD90MAC locomotives.

and its four-axle counterpart was a B30-7. Later an "A" suffix was added to indicate the use of a 12-cylinder FDL engine on models that typically would have used 16-cylinder FDL (models that always used a 12-cylinder engine did not need a suffix). Thus a B30-7A was a 12-cylinder locomotive, and B23-7 was also a 12-cylinder model.

The advent of the fuel crisis in the 1970s provided GE with a market advantage. Its four-cycle FDL engine was inherently more fuel efficient than EMD's two-cycle 645. The price of diesel fuel climbed fivefold during the 1970s. So while fuel consumption had been a minor concern in the 1960s, by 1980 it was a serious issue. GE used this to its advantage and developed even more efficient models.

EMD'S 50 SERIES

During the late 1970s EMD experimented with higher horsepower locomotives, such as its 3,500-horsepower GP40X/SD40X—the "X" standing for experimental, since these units were test beds for EMD's next product line. In 1980 it introduced its new 50-series line using the new 16-645F engine, consisting primarily of the 3,500-horsepower four-axle GP50 and six-axle SD50. Unfortunately for

EMD, this line was fraught with reliability problems, and had been introduced during a recession when hundreds of locomotives were stored nationwide because of lack of business. General Electric, on the other hand, had significantly improved its offering. Its C30-7 sold more than 1,000 units in the United States and Mexico. In 1981 it introduced the 3,600-horsepower C36-7 to the domestic market and sold 129. (Later C36-7s were rated at 3,750 horsepower, after GE upgraded its 16-cylinder FDL engine in 1985 to compete with EMD.)

MICROPROCESSOR CONTROLS

In 1983 GE captured roughly 60 percent of the domestic locomotive market, thus relegating General Motors to the number two position for the first time in modern memory. While GM recaptured the majority of the market in 1984, it would only hold it for three more years. During 1982 General Electric built a test locomotive using new micro-processor control technology. By 1984 it had refined this technology and introduced several preproduction DASH-8 locomotives for railroad testing. (GE uses all capital letters with its DASH-8 line.) Onboard computers allowed extremely tight control

Conrail operated ten GE C32-8s, which GE describes as "Classics." They were among the first American locomotives to use microprocessor controls. Conrail 6611 is seen here at Silver Springs, New York, on October 24, 1987.

on locomotive functions in order to maximize performance and fuel efficiency. This level of computer control changed the locomotive industry and brought about a whole new level of higher performance expectations. One important feature of the DASH-8 line was a modular carbody design that permitted several locomotive models to use essentially the same carbody. While notable for its pioneering use of microprocessor computer controls, GE's early DASH-8 locomotives are identified by their unique appearance: a pronounced humpback that contained dynamic braking grids and blowers, a distinctive rounded cab roof, and a chiseled, tapered, low, short hood. These preproduction DASH-8s were built concurrently with GE's Dash-7 line, and known to GE employees as "classics" to distinguish them from later production DASH-8s. In 1984 Conrail took delivery of 50 C30-7As using GE's 12-cylinder FDL engine, followed immediately by 10 C32-8s, which were rated at 3,150 horsepower and used the DASH-8 carbody. While it refined the design, GE built

very few classic DASH-8 locomotives, but Norfolk Southern and Conrail both acquired "classic" C39-8s.

General Electric introduced its "Enhanced" DASH-8 line at the end of 1987. This new production line ushered in a generation of reliable, efficient locomotives that allowed GE to quickly reclaim the largest share of the American locomotive market. Several new models were produced, the most popular being the 4,000-horsepower DASH 8-40C. It also offered a line of high-horsepower four-motor locomotives designed for high-horsepower, high-speed applications, especially on fast, long-distance, intermodal runs. This type of locomotive appealed to Conrail, Santa Fe, and Southern Pacific—lines that already operated large high-horsepower four-motor fleets.

EMD's 710G Engine

In the early 1980s EMD scrambled to regain its competitive edge and spent four years developing its new 710G engine to supplant the 1960s-era 645 engine. General Motors

Norfolk Southern C36-7 8533 ascending the Elkhorn grade looms out of the morning fog at Maybeury, West Virginia, on June 18, 1998. General Electric's later C36-7s included the dynamic braking design used on the DASH-8 line and all subsequent GE locomotives.
Tom S. Hoover

The 6,000 Horsepower Milestone

by Sean Graham-White

Since General Motors and General Electric announced in 1993 that they would be offering locomotives rated at 6,000 horsepower, the expectations were tall for the future of high-horsepower locomotives. True to form, Union Pacific, a railroad with a history of purchasing the highest-horsepower locomotives available, stepped up to the plate and ordered from both builders, with CSX and Southern Pacific quickly following suit with orders for GE's unit. The anticipation and questions concerning the 6,000-horsepower locomotives were just beginning, and as this is being written in spring of 1999, the answers are only now just arriving.

Every decade or so since diesel locomotives were introduced there has been a horsepower war. In the early days, the increases in horsepower were in the hundreds of horsepower, but today these jumps can reach 2,000 horsepower. Locomotives equipped with DC traction motors peaked at 4,400 horsepower, but the introduction of AC traction motors meant the possibility of higher numbers. Since many of the "standard" locomotives rated at 3,000 horsepower across North America were purchased during the 1970s and 1980s, their useful life spans of 20–30 years were running out. The idea that a 6,000-horsepower locomotive could replace two "standard" locomotives was a practical idea now that AC traction motors were available, but how to achieve 6,000 horsepower?

While it isn't that difficult to construct an engine that can produce 6,000 horsepower, the difficulty arises with constructing one that will fit within the constraints of a locomotive carbody and one that will not weigh significantly more than previous designs. In addition to withstanding the rigors of day-to-day railroad work, the engine must be able to deliver optimum performance in a variety of harsh conditions from the Southwestern deserts to Arctic conditions of Canada, and at a variety of altitudes from below sea level to over 10,000 feet. These are difficult conditions indeed, and both builders, after much research into the capabilities of their current designs, decided to develop completely new engines to power their 6,000-horsepower locomotives.

GM ended up going it alone in its design process. The result was the 265H—the first four-cycle design for a GM locomotive. GE partnered with Deutz MWM of Germany to develop their new engine—the HDL, also a four-cycle. Both use 16-cylinders and twin turbochargers, and have been designed to fit into roughly the same space as   previous engine models. Evaluation 6,000-horsepower engines were being tested as early as 1994 in test cells at each builder's factories. But when would they enter production and who would be the first to have one operating on a railroad?

The race was joined and development scurried along. GM kept its engine within the confines of its plants and the Association of American Railroad's test track in Pueblo, Colorado, while GE released preproduction locomotives to Union Pacific and CSX (the Southern Pacific order had been cancelled—and in 1996 SP itself had merged with UP). The promise that production of 6,000-horsepower locomotives would begin in 1997 remained as the then-distant objective for both builders. Meanwhile, in order to get a jump on deliveries of the locomotives to hold these engines, Union Pacific agreed to accept "Convertible" locomotives from both builders, and the first of these arrived in 1995. "Convertibles" are locomotives designed to accept either a 6,000-horsepower engine or the previous engine designs until the 6,000-horsepower engines become available. Initially the convertibles were equipped with the older engine designs rated at 4,300 horsepower in the GMs and 4,390 horsepower in the GEs.

The convertibles went through their paces, putting in mile after mile of service, and their numbers steadily increased. Locomotive orders from both builders intended as 6,000-horsepower units were delivered as convertibles instead. All of 1997 passed, however, as both builders were experiencing development difficulties with their engines. The 6,000-horsepower engines were completely new beasts, and each builder had to tweak their designs to allow for engineering improvements. New mechanical designs take time and in the meantime the result was even more convertible locomotives. Finally in 1998 both builders entered production of their new designs.

With the prospect of needing far fewer locomotives to move trains, issues concerning the design of 6,000-horsepower locomotives have focused on reliability and fuel efficiency. Reliability has become especially important because with fewer locomotives, if any were to fail en route, more severe delays could result. In a traditional consist, if one of four 3,000-horsepower locomotives fails then only 25 percent of the power is lost, while if one of two 6,000-horsepower locomotives fails, there is a 50 percent loss of power. Fuel efficiency is an important consideration, and the goal was to create a locomotive that can match the performance of two "standard" locomotives while using less fuel. The 6,000-horsepower locomotive designs employ onboard computers to manage the locomotive's subsystems in order to maximize locomotive efficiency and check for problems that might result in a component failure. This technology even allows the locomotive to call ahead to the next repair facility to let the maintenance people know exactly what is going wrong so they are ready to make repairs when the train arrives.

Most of the AC traction locomotives in North America are in the 4,000–4,400-horsepower range and work in coal and bulk commodity service. The 6,000-horsepower locomotives are intended for a different application. While there has been some use and testing of 6,000-horsepower locomotives in heavy service, they are really intended for intermodal and priority freight service, and Union Pacific and CSX have both placed their 6,000-horsepower units primarily into intermodal service. As for the promise of replacing two 3,000-horsepower units with one rated 6,000 horsepower, it is still too early to judge.

Union Pacific AC6000CW (UP designation C60AC) 7540 leads westbound intermodal train ZCSOA-17 (Canal Street, Chicago to Oakland, California) on the former Chicago & North Western near Elburn, Illinois, on December 17, 1998. Sean Graham-White

On July 26, 1993, a westbound Union Pacific freight negotiates Silver Zone Pass at the Arnold Loop—located in eastern Nevada—led by GE DASH8-40C 9169, followed by an SD40-2 and C36-7.

A view from the cab of a GE DASH8-40CW near Grand Island, Nebraska, shows a like locomotive rolling west with more than a mile of empty coal hoppers bound for Wyoming's Powder River Basin. The advent of the safety cab in 1989 quickly changed the face of railroading in the United States. Union Pacific was the first U.S. road to order safety cabs from both General Motors and General Electric.

had built an estimated 26,000 645 engines during its 20-year production run, but felt a new design was needed to meet modern horsepower and reliability standards. The 710G engine was largely based on the 645 design, but featured a longer piston stroke that resulted in an approximately 10 percent increase in cylinder displacement (710 cubic inches vs. 645 inches), an improved fuel injection system, and the new Model G turbocharger. The Model G featured a smoother gas flow, 15 percent greater than earlier models, resulting in a more efficient, more powerful, cleaner-burning engine.

General Motors incorporated its new engine design into several new models, of which the two most popular were the 3,800-horsepower GP60 and SD60, which superseded the troubled GP50 and SD50 models. The SD60 was introduced in 1984, and the GP60 a year later.

SAFETY CABS

Beginning in 1989, GM and GE began offering "widenose" safety cabs (known as "super cabs," among other names) as an option in response to crew safety concerns expressed by several large customers, including Union Pacific and Santa Fe. Union Pacific was the first railroad to use both GE and GM safety cabs. GE had built a prototype safety cab in 1988. But EMD was the first to sell safety cab–equipped, modern road locomotives in the United States with an order for SD60Ms for Union Pacific in 1989 (GM uses an "M" for the safety cab option; GE uses a "W"). While largely new to railroads in the United States, the concept had been around for decades, and had been a standard feature on many Canadian locomotives since the 1970s. In conjunction with the emergence of safety cabs, modern computerized desktop controls were introduced in place of conventional control stands.

In 1990 Santa Fe ordered a fleet of GP60Ms followed by a fleet of Dash 840BWs just as it was reintroducing its flashy silver and red warbonnet paint scheme (the railroad had reapplied this scheme to some FP45s in the late 1980s). These attractively painted locomotives were initially assigned to the railroad's "Super Fleet," typically employed to haul the railroad's fast, high-priority intermodal trains. Santa Fe was the only U.S. freight carrier to order four-axle locomotives with safety cabs (several passenger carriers used four-axle safety cabs, as did Canadian railroads). It was also the only carrier to order cabless GP60Bs.

In the late 1980s GM shifted primary responsibility for locomotive production from its La Grange, Illinois, facility to London, Ontario, in Canada, facilitated by new agreements eliminating tariffs between the United States and Canada. Locomotives no longer carried EMD builder's plates, and the diesel building division came under the General Motors Locomotive Group (GMLG) label. While prime movers are currently manufactured and some assembly work done at the old Electro-Motive facility, no locomotives are completed there. Due to demand that far exceeded EMD's capacity in the late 1990s, locomotives were assembled for EMD at Super Steel's Schenectady, New York, facility, Bombardier's Concarril, Mexico, plant, and Alsthom's Montreal facility. Canadian Pacific and Conrail have purchased locomotives in kit form for final assembly at company shops, with Conrail also assembling both EMD and GE locomotives for other railroads as well.

GE's DASH-9

In 1993 GE made a variety of improvements to its DASH-8 line. First it boosted the maximum horsepower to 4,135 horsepower, using a DASH-8-41CW designation. Later it offered electronic fuel injection (EFI) and split cooling as options designed to improve fuel efficiency and reduce harmful engine emissions. This was a response to more-stringent air quality standards (especially in California), coupled with a desire to achieve better performance. General Electric's EFI system replaced conventional mechanical fuel-injection systems and was designed to optimize engine performance through calculated variations in the fuel-injection timing. Split cooling uses two independent water circuits instead of one so that cooler water is used for engine intercooler, resulting in cleaner engine emissions. GE locomotives with the split cooling can be identified by thicker "wings" at the rear of the locomotive than appear on older models.

At the end of 1993, GE introduced its DASH-9 line, which reflected these developments, along with a new, high-adhesion truck design, an improved muffler to reduce sound emissions, a more ergonomic step and handrail configuration, and the boosting of engine output to 4,400 horsepower. The DASH-9 represented the pinnacle of GE's DC traction development and was introduced only a short time before the company built its first commercial AC traction locomotive as a competitor to GM's new AC traction SD70MAC.

AC REVOLUTION

The development of practical AC traction locomotives has been hyped as the most significant development since the advent of the diesel-electric locomotive itself. It represents a great technological leap in American diesel-electric development and in a very short span of time has eclipsed the use of DC traction motors for many applications.

Alternating-current technology dates back more than a century, and over the years AC traction motors have been applied to a variety of railway equipment. However, AC traction motors, despite numerous operating advantages, were not technically or economically feasible in heavy-haul North American service. The development and application of diesel-electric AC traction technology was a response to the railroads' desire for significantly more-powerful locomotives. Sophisticated microprocessor controls, advanced wheel slip systems, and electronic fuel injection contributed to the production of reliable, efficient 4,400-horsepower DC traction diesel-electric locomotives; however, this horsepower threshold was deemed the practical limit for the diesel-electric using conventional DC traction motor technology. In order to build locomotives with significantly greater power potential, the development of practical AC traction was the next logical step.

During the early 1980s, CSX component railroads Chessie System and Seaboard System ordered large numbers of EMD's 3,500-horsepower SD50s. On an extraordinarily clear morning SD50 8553 leads an eastbound loaded coal train on CSX's Mountain Subdivision (once known as the Baltimore & Ohio West End) at Oakland, Maryland.

Following pages
After a night of hard rain, the sun shines for a few moments on Southern Pacific's Cuesta Grade as an officers' special from Phoenix climbs toward San Francisco on March 23, 1993, at Serrano, California. Two brand-new GP60s lead the train; these units feature extended-range dynamic brakes—identified by the abnormally large "blisters" at the top center of the locomotives.

Above and above right
Burlington Northern was the first
American railroad to order a large
fleet of AC traction locomotives.
On May 25, 1995, just a few months
before the Burlington Northern
merged with Santa Fe, a trio of
SD70MACs wait for a crew at
Rozet, Wyoming. Burlington
Northern Santa Fe typically assigns
three SD70MACs to its Powder
River coal trains.

The HTCR "radial" truck employs
a self-steering mechanism that
significantly reduces wheel and
rail wear. This was one of several
innovations used by GM's SD70MAC.

Despite some advantages, DC traction motors are significantly more complex and require more maintenance than AC motors, which use fewer moving parts. DC motors cannot operate under full load below an established speed threshold without the risk of overheating. As a result, DC traction diesels could only exert maximum tractive effort for a very short period of time without damage to the traction motors. In locomotive terminology this is described as a "short time rating." (Maximum continuous tractive effort describes the most force a locomotive can exert at its slowest speed without risk of traction motor damage.)

AC motors, by contrast, have far greater range and are more durable because of their relative simplicity. The most significant advantage of AC motors is that they are virtually free from the overheating that plagues DC motors, so that locomotives can operate at virtually any speed under maximum load without risk of motor damage, generating significantly greater tractive effort, and hauling heavy trains at very slow speeds for extended periods. Additional benefits include greatly improved wheel slip control made possible through the advanced motor control, and vastly improved dynamic braking. DC locomotives with dynamic brakes can only use them to slow a train down to about 10 miles per hour, at which point dynamic braking has to be disengaged to prevent motor damage. Dynamic brakes on AC traction locomotives can be used to bring a train virtually to a complete stop, a feature that dramatically improves train handling.

Advances in microprocessor and semiconductor technology, permitting easier control of AC motors, overcame the main impediment to the practical application of powerful AC traction diesel-electric locomotives. The development of high amperage gate turn-off thyristors (GTOs) are the basis of inverters that convert DC power into a variety of three-phase AC output that is more readily modulated for motor control. A GTO acts like an on/off switch and converts DC power into an emulated sign wave that can be manipulated to control motor output. AC technology is being further refined to improve reliability and reduce cost. So while the GTO was integral to AC traction technology development, it is now being supplanted by new devices that are more capable, more reliable, and less expensive.

A modern AC traction diesel locomotive uses the same basic power generation arrangement employed by most American diesel-electric locomotives with AC-DC transmissions built since the 1960s, with the addition of inverters. This might seem unduly complicated, but the design yields a much more efficient locomotive. In this arrangement, the diesel engine turns an alternator that produces single-phase AC power (instead of a generator for DC power, as used in older diesel-electrics), which is then rectified to DC. The current is subsequently passed through inverters creating a three-phase AC output to the traction motors. The output from the alternator is not used to power the AC motors directly because it is generated at a single frequency that is difficult to control; it is the inverter's frequency modulation output that permits practical AC motor control.

General Motor's research into AC traction technology began in the 1970s, but it was not until the late 1980s that GM teamed up with the German electrical company Siemens AG to build its first AC locomotive test beds. After experimenting with a modified SDP40F, GM constructed two four-axle passenger locomotives designated F69PHAC for Amtrak. In 1991 and 1992, GM built four SD60MAC prototypes, incorporating AC traction technology with its successful SD60M design, along with other innovations such as the new HTCR self-steering, high-adhesion truck. In mid-1992, the SD60MACs, wearing a modified Burlington Northern paint scheme, began a nationwide tour, including extensive testing on BN in coal service.

By the early 1990s, BN was moving roughly 150 million tons of coal a year out of Wyoming's Powder River coal fields. This traffic had been growing every year since BN developed the Powder River Basin in the 1970s. BN knew that it would soon need a new fleet of locomotives, as the majority of its coal service locomotives were 3,000-horsepower SD40-2s and C30-7s built in the 1970s, and the railroad was especially interested in the possibilities of

A pair of Conrail SD80MACs shatter the silence on the afternoon October 25, 1996, as they crawl upgrade on the former Boston & Albany mainline near Middlefield, Massachusetts. These ACs can work at maximum throttle while moving along at less than five miles per hour without risking damage to traction motors. For this reason Conrail typically assigned them to the heavily graded B&A route.

AC traction. Unit reductions made possible by AC technology and proved by the SD60MACs in testing constituted considerable savings. The success of the SD60MACs persuaded Burlington Northern to purchase 350 similar AC traction locomotives from GM, and this enormous financial commitment, representing more than two-thirds of a billion dollars, provided GM with the financial resources for continued refinement of AC technology.

GM developed the SD70MAC, a 4,000-horsepower locomotive powered by a 16-cylinder 710G. While the SD70MAC is only 200 horsepower more powerful than the DC traction SD60M, its AC traction motors produce significantly greater tractive effort for moving coal trains. Using a 70:17 gear ratio, an SD60M produced 149,500 pounds of starting tractive effort (which it could only maintain for a very short time before onboard computers would cut engine output to avoid traction motor damage), and could maintain 100,000 pounds continuous tractive effort. EMD's older SD40s, which represented the majority of BN's coal fleet, could only maintain 87,150 pounds maximum continuous tractive effort. The SD70MAC, by contrast, can deliver an astounding 175,000 pounds starting tractive effort, and

On the 1996 winter solstice, Conrail SD80MAC rolls eastward across the Quaboag River east of Palmer, Massachusetts. Both SD80MAC and SD90MAC use the same 80-foot, 2-inch-long carbody, making them the longest single-unit locomotives operating in regular service in the United States (Union Pacific's DDA40Xs are longer, but non remain in regular service).

A westbound Union Pacific freight led by an SD90MAC and AC4400CW pauses at Woodbine, Iowa. Modern AC locomotives are really large. An SD90MAC is 80 feet, 2 inches long, 9 feet longer than an SD60M, and nearly 32 feet longer than an FT. GE's AC440CW is 73 feet, 2 inches long, 13 feet longer than a U25B, and 10 inches taller.

F59PHI

In 1994, General Motors Locomotive Group (which assumed most of GM's locomotive building responsibilities from the Electro-Motive Division in the late 1980s) introduced the F59PHI, a new passenger locomotive with a very distinctive "swoopy" look. This streamlined modern locomotive evolved from the F59PH, a passenger locomotive with a more conventional looking road-switcher body and safety cab. GMLG's F59PHI is powered by a 12-cylinder 710-G3B diesel engine, and uses an auxiliary diesel engine built for headend power. It features an AR15 alternator and D87BTR traction motors. Rated at 3,000 horsepower, it is capable of operating at 110 miles per hour, although rarely has an opportunity arisen for the locomotive to run faster than 79 miles per hour, the typical maximum speed for passenger trains on most American routes.

The F59PHI was specifically designed to meet the needs of the West Coast passenger rail market, which enjoyed enormous growth in the mid-1990s. California has experienced a true rail renaissance, with a number of new routes and dozens of new trains to meet growing passenger needs. The F59PHI was intended as competition for GE's GENESIS™—a high-horsepower passenger locomotive specifically engineered for Amtrak in the early 1990s (see sidebar)—while complying with California's strict air-quality emissions standards. Reducing environmentally hazardous engine emissions was accomplished by using a sophisticated microprocessor-controlled electronic fuel-injection system, and a better engine cooling system that incorporates larger water pumps and higher capacity radiators. In addition, the F59PHI's 12-cylinder engine is designed for greater fuel efficiency than earlier 16-cylinder models. It uses a streamlined "cowl" design to reduce wind resistance and to offer an improved appearance over the boxy, utilitarian designs built during the previous three decades. The rounded nose is made of a crash-resistant fiberglass stronger than the traditional "bulldog" nose used by EMD's E- and F-units. The locomotive also uses a modern "Isolated cab" (indicated by the "I" in the designation), which is separated from the rest of the locomotive with a rubber gasket, rides on rubber pads, and is attached to the locomotive body with shock-resistant stabilizers. This special construction reduces locomotive noise

General Motors' sleek, modern F59PHI is preferred power on many of Amtrak's West Coast runs. In December 1998, a nearly new F59PHI leads the **Leavenworth Snow Train** at Leavenworth, Washington, on the east slope of the Cascades. This locomotive's styling has been compared to GM's Chevy **Lumina** minivan.

within the cab by as much as 25 percent over earlier models, and minimizes vibration, giving the engine crew a smoother ride.

Amtrak has placed two orders for F59PHIs and generally uses them on medium-distance West Coast runs such as the San Jose to Sacramento *Capitols*, Oakland to Bakersfield, California, *San Joaquins,* and the tilting *Talgo* trains in the Pacific Northwest that connect Portland, Seattle, and Vancouver, British Columbia. Los Angeles MetroLink, the public operator of LA's highly successful suburban commuter trains, and Vancouver's BC Transit also employ small fleets of F59PHIs. While not yet used in large numbers, the F59PHI is one of the most distinctive looking modern locomotives in North America.

F59PHI Statistics:
Builder: GMLG
Engine: 12-cylinder 710-G3B
Horsepower: 3,000
Wheel Arrangement: B-B
Length: 58 feet, 6 inches
Total built: still in production

CSX's commitment to GE for 250 AC locomotives provided GE with the incentive to further refine its AC traction technology for commercial diesel locomotive applications. Two AC4400CWs lead an eastbound loaded coal train at Moss Run, Virginia, on the old Chesapeake & Ohio Alleghany Subdivision main line. *Tom S. Hoover*

In 1996 GE began delivering AC6000CW convertible locomotives to Union Pacific. While these used the conventional 7FDL engine rated at 4,400 horsepower, they are capable of receiving the new 7HDL 6,000-horsepower engine. A brand-new UP AC6000CW 7040 is seen working in Powder River coal service, meeting UP DASH8-40C 9303. *Tom S. Hoover*

137,000 pounds continuous tractive effort, an impressive increase over earlier locomotive designs. Based on increased tractive effort, BN would be able to replace five SD40-2s or C30-7s with just three SD70MACs. With just 12,000 horsepower, instead of 15,000 horsepower, the train might not move over the road as fast, but speed is not a paramount concern when hauling coal.

The SD70MAC incorporated other significant features that set it apart from earlier production models, including the HTCR radial truck, an adaptation of the HT-C truck (introduced with the Dash-2 line in the early 1970s). The HTCR employs a system of compression springs in place of the bolsters—typically used to transfer the weight of the locomotive from the frame to the wheels. The self-steering design is intended to reduce friction, and minimizes rail and wheel wear.

The advent of AC was prompted by a need for more-powerful locomotives, and soon after the SD70MAC had proved itself hauling coal trains, GM began producing two new models, the 5,000-horsepower SD80MAC, which uses a 20-cylinder 710G, and the SD90MAC (see 6,000-Horsepower Milestone sidebar).

GENERAL ELECTRIC AC

General Electric followed GM's lead in the development of AC traction locomotives; however, unlike GM, GE did not need to rely upon another company to provide AC electrical technology. GE has a long history with AC and developed its own system based on this experience. In the summer of 1993, GE built a single AC prototype, and by the end of that year CSX, one of GE's largest customers (and a major coal hauler), agreed to purchase 250 AC traction locomotives from GE. This large order, like BN's with GM, allowed GE to refine its AC traction locomotive technology.

Initially, GE developed a 4,400-horsepower locomotive, designated AC4400CW, but planned for the production of 6,000-horsepower locomotives (see 6,000-Horsepower Milestone sidebar). Externally the AC4400CW closely resembles its DC traction counterpart, the Dash9-44CW, except for a row of inverter cabinets behind the cab on the left-hand side of the locomotive (still sometimes referred to as the "fireman's side" in a carryover from steam days). By 1995, GE's AC customers included Chicago & North Western, Southern Pacific, Union Pacific, Canadian Pacific, Metro North, and Amtrak, in addition to CSX. The AC4400CW quickly proved one of GE's most successful new models.

GE's initial offering was slightly more powerful than GM's. GE's AC4400CW offered 400 additional horsepower per locomotive than the SD70MAC, and greater tractive effort—180,000 pounds starting and 145,000 continuous.

The P32BHs are Amtrak's only locomotives with North American Safety Cabs, commonly described as "widenose" cabs.

In late 1991, GE provided Amtrak with 22 DASH8-32BWH (Amtrak P32BH) locomotives. Two were paid for by California and regularly assigned to state-sponsored *Capitols* operating between San Jose and Sacramento. In August 1992, Amtrak 502 leads a westbound *Capitols* along San Pablo Bay at Pinole.

GENESIS™

In the early 1990s General Electric worked with Amtrak to develop an entirely new passenger locomotive design. In mid-1993, GE brought out the GENESIS Series, a decidedly modern, streamlined lightweight locomotive design using DASH 8-technology that bore no resemblance to anything else on American rails. The GENESIS uses a monocoque body construction, markedly different than earlier cowl designs because unlike a cowl, which is essentially just a shroud, the monocoque design uses the outer body shell as an integral part of the locomotive structure. This design is essentially a modern application of the full carbody design introduced with Electro-Motive's E-unit, and allows for an aerodynamic lightweight locomotive better suited for passenger applications. The GENESIS was also one of the first American locomotives in decades to be designed with aesthetic considerations in mind. Since the utilitarian road switcher became the dominant locomotive type, locomotive styling had played a minor role in new designs. Utility, performance, and safety have been the primary concerns, while aesthetic considerations were typically limited to paint scheme variations. While the shape and design of GENESIS were intended to be visually pleasing while conveying a modern appearance, the result has proved to be one of the most controversial-looking locomotives in recent memory. It has won design awards, but has also been heavily criticized for its unusual appearance.

The first GENESIS group, designated DASH8-40BPH (P40BH by Amtrak), using a 16-cylinder 7FDL engine, consists of four-axle locomotives rated at 4,000 horsepower and designed for a top speed of 103 miles per hour. They are 14 feet, 6 inches tall and 69 feet long—slightly longer, but with a lower profile, than Amtrak's ubiquitous F40. These are numbered in the 800 series, and are typically assigned to Amtrak's western trains.

The second group of GENESIS comprises 3,200-horsepower, dual-mode diesel-electrics—electrics designed for third-rail operation in the New York terminal area. They are specifically designed to replace aging

Metro-North operates a small fleet of dual-mode GENESIS P32AC-DMs on its suburban commuter trains out of Grand Central Terminal. On the evening of September 4, 1997, P32AC-DM 202 races along the Hudson River near Breakneck Ridge toward Poughkeepsie with a loaded commuter train.

EMD FL9s (see FL9 sidebar), which have reached the end of their useful life. Designated P32AC-DM (GE has adopted Amtrak's simpler designation system), these locomotives appear similar to other GENESIS types but are very different locomotives. In addition to their third-rail shoes, the P32AC-DMs use AC rather than DC traction motors, feature a 12-cylinder 7FDL engine, and are designed for a top speed of 110 miles per hour (60 miles per hour top speed using third rail). This specialized locomotive type was ordered by both Amtrak and Metro-North. Amtrak's P32AC-DMs are numbered in the 700 series and used exclusively on Empire Corridor trains originating from new tunnel connections at Pennsylvania Station, New York.

Beginning in Autumn 1996, Amtrak began receiving a third GENESIS type from GE, designated P42DCs. These closely resemble the first two types, but are more powerful, generating 4,250 horsepower using DC traction motors. Amtrak assigned these locomotive low road numbers, beginning with 1, and they are used in long-distance passenger service all over the United States, often mixed with the 800 series units.

Over the course of just a few years the GENESIS has displaced the F40PH as Amtrak's standard locomotive. They can now be found hauling the Boston section of *Lake Shore Limited* over the Berkshire Hills of western Massachusetts, racing the *California Zephyr* across the Nebraska plains, or bringing the *Empire Builder* over the Rocky Mountains in Montana.

P32AC-DM Statistics:
Builder: General Electric
Engine: 12-cylinder 7FLD
Horsepower: 3,200
Wheel Arrangement: B-B
Length: 69 feet
Total built: still in production

General Electric's AC's differ from GM's in some fundamental ways. GM uses just two inverters per locomotive, one for each truck, while GE uses six inverters per locomotive, one for each axle. This gives GE locomotives added reliability in the case of inverter failure. Where a GM locomotive loses roughly 40 percent of tractive effort in the event of an inverter failure (the second inverter compensates partially for a shutdown), GE just loses a fraction of its tractive effort, and can maintain 4,400 horsepower using just five inverters in most situations. The inverters generate an enormous quantity of heat, which GE disperses with an air-cooling system, while GM uses a liquid-cooling system. Initially GE did not use self-steering trucks and instead relied on the high-adhesion truck designed for its DASH-9 line. Later it responded to customer interest, and developed a steerable truck option. Compared to the SD70MAC, the AC4400CW has a distinct advantage in dynamic braking ability, although the SD80MAC is comparable.

THE FUTURE OF DC TRACTION

Despite an intense interest in AC traction locomotives, the technology has by no means dominated new locomotive acquisitions. Both GM and GE continue to build a large number of high-horsepower DC traction locomotives. GM offers its 4,000-horsepower SD70 and 4,300-horsepower SD75 with several different cab options; a few lines still prefer conventional cabs. General Electric continues to build DC traction DASH-9's for the North American market, and a variety of DC traction locomotives for the international market. While AC traction has many advantages for moving heavy trains, these must be weighed against the significantly greater cost of AC locomotives—roughly a half-million dollars more per unit. Norfolk Southern and Canadian National have not expressed interest in purchasing AC traction, and remain loyal to conventional DC power. Even Burlington Northern Santa Fe, which has been one of the greatest proponents for AC power in heavy service, continues to buy new DC locomotives for its general merchandise and intermodal freight. Norfolk & Western was the last major railroad in the United States to give up on steam and it is interesting that Norfolk Southern, the corporate successor to Norfolk & Western, has exhibited a similarly cautious approach toward AC power.

Burlington Northern SD60M 1991 was specially painted to commemorate Operation Desert Storm. On July 12, 1994, it leads a westbound empty coal train through Beach, North Dakota, against the backdrop of a tremendous thunderstorm raging along the Missouri River. Burlington Northern based its SD60Ms at Glendive, Montana, and used them primarily in Power River Coal service.

In 1979 EMD built four 3,500 SD40X locomotives that essentially used SD50 components on an SD40-2 frame. This was an interim model, built just before the SD50 went into regular production. On January 20, 1996, Kansas City Southern SD40X 703 leads a leased locomotive from MPI (Morrison-Knudsen) up the approach to the Mississippi River bridge at Baton Rouge, Louisiana. In the 1990s, many railroads relied on lease fleets to make up for short-term locomotive shortages.

Opposite, top
Despite a North American trend toward AC traction, Canadian National has been a staunch adherent to traditional DC traction, buying hundreds of GM SD70I and SD75I locomotives. These locomotives use GM's "Isolated cab," identified by the uneven nose taper. On the afternoon of June 24, 1996, a pair of clean SD70Is lead a westbound CN freight over BNSF tracks at Steward, Illinois. For a few years CN used a BNSF routing for its Chicago-Twin Cities traffic.

Opposite, bottom
A loaded Burlington Northern coal train led by GE-built C30-7 5074 at Edgemont, South Dakota, on May 26, 1995. BN had the largest fleet of C30-7s, GE's 3,000-horsepower six-motor unit designed to compete with EMD's successful SD40-2, and regularly assigned both models to Powder River coal service.

MODERN PASSENGER LOCOMOTIVES

In the last 30 years most North American railroads were relieved of their passenger obligations by various governmental agencies. In 1971 Amtrak assumed operation of most American intercity passenger services; similarly in 1978, VIA Rail assumed the passenger responsibilities of Canadian National and Canadian Pacific. By the mid-1980s, most suburban commuter rail operations were operated by a variety of local and regional agencies. During this time the majority of traditional passenger locomotives (mostly EMD Es and Fs) were retired or remanufactured.

In the early 1970s, Amtrak needed a new fleet of locomotives and looked to EMD and GE for new designs. At that time Amtrak's future seemed particularly uncertain, and its early locomotives were designed for easy conversion to freight service should Amtrak cease passenger operations. Initially, EMD built a fleet of SDP40Fs, essentially a cowl version of the passenger service SDP40, which closely resembled FP45s built a few years earlier for Santa Fe. They were 3,000-horsepower locomotives powered by a 16-cylinder 645, and featured a boiler and steam equipment for passenger cars, which employed steam heat at that time (a carryover from the steam era). Amtrak acquired 150 SDP40Fs, intending them primarily for long-distance passenger runs.

In 1976, Amtrak acquired a small fleet of 3,000-horsepower F40PHs, a cowl version of the successful GP40-2. The F40PHs, numbered in the 200 series to commemorate the nation's bicentennial, were originally intended for short passenger runs and were equipped with electric headend power for use with new Budd-built Amfleet cars. The SDP40Fs had experienced a rash of serious derailments, believed to have stemmed from flaws in the trucks—a new variation of the HT-C design. Concerns over these derailments escalated, and furthermore, Amtrak was looking to phase out steam-heated equipment in favor of headend electric power. As a result, Amtrak asked EMD to rebuild most of the SDP40Fs into F40PHs designed for long-distance runs. These F40s used a variety of SDP40F parts, and featured higher capacity fuel tanks than the first F40PHs. The SDP40F was quietly phased out after just a few years, and the F40PH became Amtrak's standard passenger locomotive for nearly two decades. Later it was adopted by a number of other passenger carriers, including VIA Rail. EMD built many F40 variations over the years, as well as other passenger types, to suit the specific needs of its customers.

In the 1990s, GM developed a new passenger locomotive designated the F59PHI (see sidebar). GM has also developed two modern types of passenger locomotive for the Long Island Rail Road, including a dual mode locomotive for service into New York's Penn Station tunnels.

During the 1960s, 1970s, and 1980s, General Electric was far less successful in the passenger locomotive market than EMD. In the late 1960s it built a few passenger locomotives for Santa Fe—U28CGs in a road-switcher carbody, and U30CGs in a cowl configuration. Between 1970 and 1973 it built 32 U34CHs in a road-switcher configuration for Erie-Lackawanna commuter services, and in 1975 and 1976 it built 25 P30CHs in a cowl configuration for Amtrak. At the

end of 1991 GE built 22 four-motor passenger locomotives with safety cabs for Amtrak, designated DASH8-32BWH (Amtrak designates them P32BH). These locomotives closely resemble DASH8-40BWs built for Santa Fe. The DASH8-32BWH was a prelude to the more radical GENE-SIS™ passenger locomotive (see GENESIS sidebar) that has become Amtrak's standard passenger locomotive.

A STRONG FUTURE

The American diesel locomotive has come a long way from its earliest applications as slow speed switchers in smoke-free zones. Horsepower and fuel efficiency have been steadily improved by the implementation of increasingly better designs. Since the 1950s diesel-electric locomotives have hauled the vast majority of American trains, and American-designed diesel-electrics are used by railways around the world (one of our few remaining profitable export products). Today, American freight railroads are car-

HOUSTON'S SWITCHERS ON THE PROWL

by Sean Graham-White

Production of switcher locomotives by the two major manufacturers, General Motors and General Electric, ended in the late 1980s following a perceived decline in the new switcher market. While many railroads continued to rely on switchers constructed during the past four decades, others felt a need for an efficient modern switcher that was no longer available from GM or GE. So in 1992, MK Rail, a long-time contract rebuilder and remanufacturer of road locomotives, announced its own line of switchers to fill this gap in the market. Initially, two different models were introduced, MK1200G and MK1500D. Both shared many integral components, the principal difference between them being fuel. The MK1200G is designed to burn liquefied natural gas (LNG) and generates 1,200 horsepower, making it the first commercially available natural gas switcher in North America. So far only Union Pacific and Santa Fe have acquired this model, both for operation in southern California territory in order to test the differences between LNG and diesel fuel exhaust emissions. Southern California has some of the strictest exhaust emissions in the nation.

The MK1500D, which burns traditional diesel fuel, has proved more successful. The MK1500D has sold to several railroads; the largest operator is the Port Terminal Railway Association (PTRA) of Houston, which was created in 1924 by 12 area railroads to serve industries along the Houston ship channel. However, as a result of railroad mergers, the PTRA is now owned by just two companies, Burlington Northern Santa Fe and Union Pacific. PTRA purchased 24 MK1500Ds in 1996 to replace 30 older, inefficient "hand-me-down" locomotives supplied by its owner railroads. These locomotives were so unreliable that 30 were maintained to do the work of 23. Of the 24 MK1500Ds used today, only one is a spare. Using 23 locomotives

Port Terminal Railway Association of Houston operates a fleet of 24 MK1500D switchers. MK Rail (now Boise Locomotive Company), designed a switcher to fill a market niche ignored by GM and GE in recent years. **Sean Graham-White**

instead of 30 units has resulted in significant cost savings.

The MK1500D is powered by a turbocharged 12-cylinder Caterpillar engine, which is a very fuel-efficient, quiet engine that generates minimal harmful exhaust, yet produces 1,375 horsepower. MK advertised the MK1500D as 12 percent more efficient than other switchers, but PTRA tests found them 17 percent more efficient than older switchers. PRTA saved 600,000 gallons of fuel in one year by using MK1500Ds in their first year of operation. One of the main reasons for the units' fuel efficiency is SmartStart—which shuts the locomotive down after 30 minutes if no work is being done (however a safety feature will keep the engine running if the temperature falls below 40 degrees or the main air reservoir falls below 90 pounds). Microprocessors onboard the MK1500D control numerous other functions, including traction control and sanding. The locomotives typically spend an average of 20 hours a day pulling trains along the ship channel and switching industries, and rarely reach speeds faster than 20 miles per hour. PTRA has found that one MK1500D can haul 10,000 tons over level terrain, an impressive statistic for a switcher. Aside from all the modern technology and efficiencies introduced by the MK switchers, if you ask the crews in Houston what their favorite piece of equipment is, they would say the air conditioning!

MK1500D Statistics:
Builder: MK Rail (now Boise Locomotive Company)
Engine: 12-cylinder Caterpillar 3512
Horsepower: 1,375
Wheel Arrangement: B-B
Length: 56 feet, 2 inches
Total built: still in production

rying record loads, requiring ever greater amounts of power. The advent of AC locomotives has created a whole new demand for locomotives, as railroads gradually place AC locomotives in premier service. The locomotive market remains healthy, and in 1999 General Electric was anticipating a record year for locomotive construction. However, because both builders have been constructing large numbers of modern high-horsepower locomotives at a rapid rate in the late 1990s, the market demand for new power will likely ebb. But the diesel has no serious rival in the American market, and barring the unforeseen, it would appear the diesel-electric will remain the choice railway motive power for many years to come.

Right
In September 1998, Amtrak P42 15 leads the *Southwest Chief* eastbound east of Wagon Mound, New Mexico, on the old Santa Fe mainline. This is one of three varieties of GENESIS locomotives employed by Amtrak.

A Cal-Train F40PH departs San Francisco with a "Commute" bound for San Jose. The F40PH is essentially an adaptation of the successful GP40-2 road switcher for passenger service. The type was first used by Amtrak in 1976, and became the standard American passenger locomotive for nearly two decades.

Following page
In September 1990, four brand-new GP60Ms in the sparkling "warbonnet" scheme lead Santa Fe's hot 199 intermodal train westward through Franklin Canyon near Christie—only a few miles away from its terminus at Richmond, California. The GP60Ms were Santa Fe's first locomotives equipped with safety cabs. Santa Fe was one of the last American railroads to buy a large fleet of high-horsepower four-motor locomotives, assigning them to its "Super fleet" intermodal service.

BIBLIOGRAPHY

BOOKS

Alymer-Small, Sidney. *The Art of Railroading, Vol. VIII*. Chicago: Railway Publication Society, 1908.

Anderson, Norman E., and C. G. MacDermot. *PA4 Locomotives*. Burlingame, Calif.: Chatham Publishing Co., 1978.

Armstrong, John H. *The Railroad—What It Is, What It Does*. Omaha, Neb.: Simmons-Boardman, 1982.

Bruce, Alfred W. *The Steam Locomotive in America*. New York: Norton, 1952.

Burch, Edward P. *Electric Traction for Railway Trains*. New York: McGraw-Hill Book Co., 1911.

Bush, Donald, J. *The Streamlined Decade*. New York: George Braziller, 1975.

Churella, Albert J. *From Steam to Diesel*. Princeton, N.J.: Princeton University Press, 1998.

Condit, Carl. *Port of New York, Vols. 1 & 2*. Chicago: University of Chicago Press, 1980, 1981.

Diemer, Hugo. *Self-propelled Railway Cars*. Chicago, 1910.

Dolzall, Gary W., and Stephen F. Dolzall. *Baldwin Diesel Locomotives*. Milwaukee, Wis.: Kalmbach, 1984.

Drury, George H. *Guide to North American Steam Locomotives*. Waukesha, Wis.: Kalmbach, 1993.

Farrington, S. Kip, Jr. *Railroads at War*. New York: Coward-McCann, Inc., 1944.

Farrington, S. Kip, Jr. *Railroading the Modern Way*. New York: Coward-McCann, Inc., 1951.

Garmany, John B. *Southern Pacific Dieselization*. Edmonds, Wash.:Pacific Fast Mail, 1985.

Garrett, Colin. *The World Encyclopedia of Locomotives*. London, 1997.

General Motors. *Electro-Motive Division Operating Manual No. 2300*. La Grange, Ill.: General Motors, 1945.

Gregg, Newton K. *Train Shed Cyclopedia No. 20*. Novato, Calif., 1974.

Harlow, Alvin F. *The Road of the Century*. New York: Creative Age Press, Inc., 1947.

Haut, F.J.G. *The Pictorial History of Electric Locomotives*. Cranbury, N.J.: A.S. Barnes, 1970.

Herrick, Albert, B. *Practical Electric Railway Hand Book*. New York: McGraw Publishing Co., 1906.

Hofsommer, Don. L. *Southern Pacific 1900-1985*. College Station, Texas: Texas A&M University, 1986.

Jennison, Brian, and Victor Neves. *Southern Pacific Oregon Division*. Mukilteo, Wash.: Hundman Publishing Co., 1997.

Kalmbach, A.C. *Railroad Panorama*. Milwaukee, Wis.: Kalmbach, 1944.

Keilty, Edmund. *Interurbans Without Wires*. Glendale, Calif.: Interurbans Publications, 1979.

Kiefer, P.W. *A Practical Evaluation of Railroad Motive Power*. New York: Steam Locomotive Research, 1948.

Kirkland, John F. *Dawn of the Diesel Age*. Glendale, Calif.: Interurbans Publications, 1983.

Kirkland, John F. *The Diesel Builders, Vols. I, II, and III*. Pasadena, Calif.: Interurbans Press, 1994.

Klein, Maury. *Union Pacific, Vol. II*. New York: Doubleday & Co., 1989.

Marre, Louis A. *Rock Island Diesel Locomotives*. Cincinnati, Ohio: Railfax, 1982.

Marre, Louis A., and Jerry A. Pinkepank. *The Contemporary Diesel Spotter's Guide*. Milwaukee, Wis.: Kalmbach, 1985.

Marre, Louis A. *Diesel Locomotives: The First 50 Years*. Waukesha, Wis.: Kalmbach, 1995.

Middleton, William D. *When the Steam Railroads Electrified*. Milwaukee, Wis.: Kalmbach, 1974.

Middleton, William D. *Grand Central . . . the World's Greatest Railway Terminal*. San Marino, Calif.: Golden West Books, 1977.

Morgan, David P. *Steam's Finest Hour*. Milwaukee, Wis.: Kalmback, 1959.

Mulhearn, Daniel J., and John R. Taibi. *General Motors' F-Units*. New York: Quadrant Press, 1982.

Pinkepank, Jerry A. *The Second Diesel Spotter's Guide*. Milwaukee, Wis.: Kalmbach, 1973.

Ransome-Wallis, P. *World Railway Locomotives*. New York: Hawthorn Books Inc., 1959.

Reck, Franklin M. *On Time. Electro-Motive Division of General Motors*. 1948.

Reck, Franklin M. *The Dilworth Story*. New York: McGraw-Hill, 1954.

Rose, Joseph R. *American Wartime Transportation*. New York, 1953.

Signor, John R. *Rails in the Shadow of Mt. Shasta*. San Diego: Howell-North Book, 1982.

Signor, John R. *Tehachapi*. San Marino, Calif.: Golden West Books, 1983.

Signor, John R. *Donner Pass: Southern Pacific's Sierra Crossing*. San Marino, Calif.: Golden West Books, 1985.

Signor, John R. *The Los Angeles and Salt Lake Railroad Company*. San Marino, Calif.: Golden West Books, 1988.

Signor, John R. *Beaumont Hill*. San Marino, Calif.: Golden West Books, 1990.

Sillcox, Lewis K. *Mastering Momentum*. New York: Simmons-Boardman Pub. Corp., 1955.

Solomon, Brian. *Trains of the Old West*. New York: Metrobooks, 1998.

Solomon, Brian. *The American Steam Locomotive*. Osceola, Wis.: MBI Publishing Co., 1998.

Staff, Virgil. *D-Day on the Western Pacific*. Glendale, Calif.: Interurban Press, 1982.

Strapac, Joseph A. *Southern Pacific Motive Power Annual 1971*. Burlingame, Calif., 1971.

Strapac, Joseph A. *Southern Pacific Review 1981*. Huntington Beach, Calif.: Railway & Locomotive Historical Society, 1982.

Strapac, Joseph A. *Southern Pacific Review 1952–1982*. Huntington Beach, Calif.: Railway & Locomotive Historical Society, 1983.

Strapac, Joseph A. *Southern Pacific Review 1953–1985*. Huntington Beach, Calif.: Railway & Locomotive Historical Society, 1986.

Staufer, Alvin F. *New York Central's Early Power 1831–1916*. Medina, Ohio: Alvin F. Staufer, 1967.

Staufer, Alvin F., and Edward L. May. *New York Central's Later Power 1910-1968*. Medina, Ohio: Alfin F. Staufer, 1981.

Staufer, Alvin F. *Pennsy Power III*. Medina, Ohio: Alfin F. Staufer, 1968.

BROCHURES

Peck, David. "Alco FA-2." Hundman Publishing, Edmonds, Wash. (no date).

General Electric. "GENESIS." Erie, Pa. (1993?).

General Electric. "GE Locomotives." (no date).

Alco-Méditerranée S.A.R.L. "Alco 251 Diesels." Paris, France (no date).

PERIODICALS

Locomotive & Railway Preservation. Waukesha, Wis. (no longer published).

RailNews. Waukesha, Wis.

Railroad History, formerly *Railway and Locomotive Historical Society Bulletin*. Boston, Mass.

Official Guide to the Railways. New York.

Southern Pacific Bulletin. San Francisco.

Trains. Waukesha, Wis.

Vintage Rails. Waukesha, Wis.

INDEX